STRUCTURE PHENOMENOLOGY

ALSO AVAILABLE FROM BLOOMSBURY

Crisis and Husserlian Phenomenology: A Reflection on Awakened Subjectivity, Kenneth Knies

Hermeneutics and Phenomenology: Figures and Themes, ed. Saulius Geniusas and Paul Fairfield

Phenomenology and the Social Context of Psychiatry: Social Relations, Psychopathology, and Husserl's Philosophy, ed. Magnus Englander

STRUCTURE PHENOMENOLOGY

Preconscious Formation in the Epistemic Disclosure of Reality

HERBERT WITZENMANN

Edited by Johannes Wagemann

Translated by Johannes Wagemann and Troy Vine

BLOOMSBURY ACADEMIC

LONDON • NEW YORK • OXFORD • NEW DELHI • SYDNEY

BLOOMSBURY ACADEMIC
Bloomsbury Publishing Plc
50 Bedford Square, London, WC1B 3DP, UK
1385 Broadway, New York, NY 10018, USA
29 Earlsfort Terrace, Dublin 2, Ireland

BLOOMSBURY, BLOOMSBURY ACADEMIC and the Diana logo are trademarks of Bloomsbury Publishing Plc

First published in 1983 in Germany as *Strukturphänomenologie: Vorbewusstes Gestaltbilden im erkennenden Wirklichkeitenthüllen* by Gideon Spicker Verlag

First published in Great Britain 2022
This paperback edition published in 2024

Copyright © Alanus Hochschule, Johannes Wagemann and Troy Vine, 2022

Copyright Editorial Introduction © Johannes Wagemann, 2022

Johannes Wagemann has asserted his right under the Copyright, Designs and Patents Act, 1988, to be identified as Editor of this work.

For legal purposes the Acknowledgments on pp. viii–xi constitute an extension of this copyright page.

Series design by Charlotte Daniels
Cover image © Johannes Wagemann

This work is published open access subject to a Creative Commons Attribution-NonCommercial-NoDerivatives 3.0 licence (CC BY-NC-ND 3.0, https://creativecommons.org/licenses/by-nc-nd/3.0/). You may re-use, distribute, and reproduce this work in any medium for non-commercial purposes, provided you give attribution to the copyright holder and the publisher and provide a link to the Creative Commons licence.

Bloomsbury Publishing Plc does not have any control over, or responsibility for, any third-party websites referred to or in this book. All internet addresses given in this book were correct at the time of going to press. The author and publisher regret any inconvenience caused if addresses have changed or sites have ceased to exist, but can accept no responsibility for any such changes.

A catalogue record for this book is available from the British Library.

A catalog record for this book is available from the Library of Congress.

ISBN:	HB:	978-1-3502-7043-5
	PB:	978-1-3502-7047-3
	ePDF:	978-1-3502-7044-2
	eBook:	978-1-3502-7045-9

Typeset by Integra Software Services Pvt. Ltd.

To find out more about our authors and books visit www.bloomsbury.com and sign up for our newsletters.

CONTENTS

List of Figures vii

Editorial Foreword and Acknowledgments viii

Editorial Introduction to Structure Phenomenology xii

    1. Biographical Notes xv
    2. The Role of Introspection xvii
    3. Intentionality and the Basic Structure xxii
    4. The Deposited Memory Layer xxxii
    5. Reality Access and Ontological Stratification xxxix
    6. Critical Remarks xlix
    7. Reception and Further Development of Witzenmann's Structure Phenomenology liv

Structure Phenomenology lviii

Foreword lix

    Introduction: Demarcation and Structure 1

1 The Basic Structure 5

    1.1 Mistaken Conceptions of the Relation between Consciousness and Object 5
    1.2 The Basic Structure in the Light of Rudolf Steiner's Epistemology 9
    1.3 Explanatory Remarks 13

2 The Crucial Difficulty. The Problem of Generation 17

3 The Proposed Solution 31

- 3.1 Thinking Act and Thought Content (Evidence) 31
- 3.2 Further Elucidation on This Approach to a Solution 33
- 3.3 Formation of Reality and Beings 38
- 3.4 The Sub-temporal and Super-temporal 44
- 3.5 Thinking Act and Self-consciousness (the "I"). The Concept of Observation 46
- 3.6 The Solution to the Problem of Memory 49
- 3.7 The Deposited Memory Layer. The Concept of Objectivity. The Gaze behind the Veil 54
- 3.8 The Concept of Presence 63
- 3.9 Structural and Functional Remembering 71
- 3.10 The Paradox of Self-giving. The Self-forgetfulness of Supposing 73
- 3.11 Results of the Structure-Phenomenological Exploration of the Contents of Consciousness 75

4 The Significance of Structure Phenomenology 83

Advice for the Reader 93

Bibliography 97

Index 107

LIST OF FIGURES

1 Forms of Intentionality and Intentional Content — xxix
2 The Schema of Structure Phenomenology — 81

EDITORIAL FOREWORD AND ACKNOWLEDGMENTS

This first English edition of Herbert Witzenmann's (1905–1988) central work *Structure Phenomenology* is intended not only to make his thought accessible to the English-speaking world but also to show that this relatively unknown approach can contribute to current, widespread debates in philosophy and psychology and, especially, to the emerging field of first-person consciousness research. While the subject-specific aspects of this book will be outlined in an editorial introduction following this foreword, the details of the translation and publication are described here. One of my first projects as an assistant professor for consciousness research at Alanus University in summer 2014 was to translate Witzenmann's *Strukturphänomenologie* (1983),[1] which had proved to be an important conceptual compass to me during the previous twenty years, particularly while working on my dissertation until 2009. I then met Dr. Troy Vine, an English speaker well versed in philosophy, who already knew the book and was interested in collaborating on a translation. After having raised the necessary funds, we started in 2015 with a first draft translation by Troy which we extensively, sentence per sentence, discussed and refined—a process that over the following two years eventually led to three more versions, until I had the impression that it was moving

---

[1]Witzenmann, 1983a

toward a consistent result. In the next step, the text was reviewed by Donald Goodwin which, due to the complex work and his very conscientious commitment, took almost another year. Finally, I incorporated his corrections and suggestions and completed the work on the text corpus.

The original book is not easy to read, even for German-speaking scholars, and so it is not surprising that the English translation of the relatively short text of about hundred pages took over four years to produce. This is certainly due on the one hand to the complex topic of structure phenomenology, but on the other hand it also results from Witzenmann's elaborate use of language including neologisms for which we have struggled for suitable translations. Moreover, Witzenmann's style is predominantly characterized by a sober, scientific precision, but in some places, especially toward the end of the book, it also contains some almost poetic formulations which did not make the translation any easier. Against this background, we have tried, on the one hand, to work out a translation close to the text to make Witzenmann's challenging language style experienceable in English. On the other hand, we have deviated from the original sentence structure in places where it seemed unavoidable with a view to intelligibility. In all cases, the fundamental orientation for translation was the methodological challenge presented by structure phenomenology inasmuch as it understands language not only as a symbolic representation of abstract argumentation, but also uses it to direct attention and stimulate activity referring to the reader's own mental processes. Therefore, as far as possible we had to enter into these processes and phenomena ourselves and to clarify in dialogue how best to express them in English. This may illustrate that the translated version of the book remains a workbook which is waiting for exploration and discussion by interested researchers.

Since Witzenmann deviated from present-day academic practice insofar as he did not consistently provide references to literature on scientific and philosophical approaches he discussed or certain terms he used, I have decided to add editorial references and brief comments at appropriate places in the book (marked by square brackets [...]). In order not to further complicate the readability of the already difficult text, I have limited myself to the most essential information, often only to the literature reference and kept it as short as possible. These footnotes refer to sources that Witzenmann explicitly mentioned in the text and, selected by me, to scholarly work that might have been known to Witzenmann when he wrote the book, or to related works by him. Instead of confusing the original text with too many annotations, central topics of structure phenomenology are addressed and contextualized, also with reference to contemporary approaches, in the following introduction. However, in order to facilitate a direct reference to the book text, key terms in the introduction are italicized on first mention and relevant quotations from the book are provided; for illustration purposes, some further passages from the text are also quoted in the introduction. With regard to the original text, most, but not all, italics have been adopted. In addition, all footnotes in the original text have been included; the literature mentioned there by Witzenmann was integrated into the editorial bibliography.

I want to close these remarks by giving special thanks to Troy Vine for his qualified, subtle and perseverant collaboration on the translation of the main text of this book and to Donald Goodwin for his very solid, careful, and consistent review and proofreading of both the main text and the introduction. The financial resources for this work were generously provided by the research funding of the Anthroposophical Society in Germany (ASG) and by the GLS Treuhand Foundation, Open Access funding was generously provided by ASG, Sylvia Witzenmann and Dorothea Paschen, to all of whom I extend my sincere thanks. For reading the translated text and giving inspiring comments, I am grateful to Fergus Anderson, Terje Sparby, Manfred Schwenzfeier, and Peter Stewart, and I particularly thank Christopher Gutland for discussing some issues about Husserl with me. Furthermore, I want to extend many thanks to Götz Rehn and Klaus Hartmann of the Herbert Witzenmann Foundation for the license to translate and publish this work. Last not least, I want to thank three anonymous reviewers whose constructive feedback helped to further improve the editorial introduction, as well as Liza Thompson and Lucy Russell at Bloomsbury for the smooth and supportive production process.

EDITORIAL INTRODUCTION TO STRUCTURE PHENOMENOLOGY

Based on Brentano's and Husserl's seminal work, phenomenology was established in the twentieth century alongside and distinct from other philosophical fields, such as ontology, epistemology, and ethics. However, since phenomenology is not just another philosophical topic, but a basic method of knowledge implicitly practiced since time immemorial, it appears characteristic that it developed not only in terms of philosophical undercurrents, as personified in Husserl's successors such as Heidegger, Sartre, Merleau-Ponty, and others, but also regarding other scientific disciplines. From a more general epistemological point of view, it can be said that every academic discipline requires certain aspects of phenomenological investigation, particularly in the initial stages of the subject-specific procedures when the objects of research are first inspected and defined as such at all.[2] Only based on this initial exploration and subsequent abstraction from phenomenal lifeworld experience can the further steps of scientific research routines be conducted. This includes the invention of measuring devices, the construction of hypothetical models and theories as well as the formulation of research questions and their validation, foremost, in the natural sciences, in mathematized and

---

[2]Crease, 1993; Kockelmans & Kisiel, 1970; Stumpf, 1907

experimental form. However, a similar process of abstraction from lifeworld experience also takes place in the humanities via hermeneutic interpretation, formal argumentation, and logical inference—and thus of course also in philosophy itself. This parallelism points to the ambivalent relationship of phenomenology to *all* forms of academic endeavor: On the one hand, phenomenology now appears to have been incorporated into the field of academic philosophy or to have become an implicit or explicit methodological side-aspect of other disciplines. On the other hand, phenomenology seems to provide essential prerequisites for any kind of knowledge acquisition and hence could be deemed to have a fundamental significance in, as well as beyond, the field of academic philosophy, even though this significance is mostly underappreciated. This claim, however, expressed by Husserl as a critical rejection of objectivistic science and aspiring to ground all science through phenomenology, raises the delicate question as to whether and how phenomenology would be really able to methodologically ground itself to be adequately prepared for this challenge regarding other disciplines.[3]

It is well known that Husserl's answers to this question in terms of his phenomenological method and a "universally, apodictically grounded and grounding science" strengthened the acceptance of subjective experience in twentieth-century philosophy, but also involved a kind of transcendental idealism[4]. While the former has indeed led to an increased interest in descriptive phenomenology, for example in psychology and the cognitive sciences, the latter has been critically questioned and marginalized in relation to the

---

[3]Husserl, 1970
[4]Husserl, 1970, p. 338

more pragmatic aspects of phenomenology.[5] Thus, the universalist concern of the phenomenological project, which was also articulated in Brentano's prioritization of a first-person method in descriptive psychology—which he regarded as an exact science—over empirical psychology, has remained unfulfilled up to now.[6] In the intellectual milieu of today's pluralism and relativism, this is not conspicuous, but in view of unsolved basic problems in science it can make us think: Will it eventually be possible to understand the nature of matter in terms of smaller and smaller particles, which are sought in huge accelerators with larger and larger amounts of energy? Does it make sense to reduce organic life to physical or biochemical measures? How is it supposed to have developed from inorganic matter? Is there a constitutive relationship between brain processes and phenomenal consciousness and if so, how can it be understood? Of course, it would be audacious to expect comprehensive answers to these questions from today's phenomenology alone—but perhaps phenomenology, in its impartial orientation to the things as they initially appear and further develop in human consciousness, can offer more than methodological auxiliary techniques or one-sided idealist conceptions.

This is the point at which Herbert Witzenmann's structure phenomenology comes into play since he placed it in the broader context of a transdisciplinary methodological foundation of science, on the one hand, and a synoptic approach to epistemology and ontology, on the other hand. One reason why Witzenmann has so far been so sparsely received may be the fact that his approach, at least in its essential features, cannot be simply traced back to the Husserlian

---

[5]Gallagher & Schmicking, 2010; Giorgi, 2009
[6]Brentano, 1995

tradition, but rather to Johann Wolfgang Goethe's (1749–1832) method of natural research and its subsequent elaboration by Rudolf Steiner (1861–1925) to a spiritually oriented consciousness phenomenology or "anthroposophy".[7] Nevertheless, many implicit references to Husserl's and other phenomenological thought appear in Witzenmann's work, which on closer analysis prove to be in part connections but often also independent extensions. In order to elucidate these and other aspects, the following introduction begins with some biographical notes on Witzenmann (1) and continues with a discussion of four key topics of structure phenomenology; these are intended as exemplary illustrations of some of the similarities and differences in relation to Husserlian phenomenology and to other philosophical lines of thought: The role of introspection (2), intentionality and the basic structure (3), the deposited memory layer (4), reality access and ontological stratification (5). This, of course, can only give a first outline and is far from claiming completeness, which rather requires extensive further research. In this direction, after some critical remarks (6), there are some first links to and further developments of Witzenmann's structure phenomenology which are summarized at the end of this introduction (7).

1. Biographical Notes

Originally, Witzenmann's book *Strukturphänomenologie* was published in 1983 in his late creative period as a revised and extended version of a series of lectures that he held at the Ruhr-Universität

---

[7] For a comparison of the Goethean and Husserlian approaches to phenomenology, see Weik, 2016.

Bochum. However, Herbert Witzenmann (1905–1988) was not a philosopher in the typical academic sense. Gifted with wide interests and profound talents, especially in music, literature, and poetry, he went through a rich university education in the fields of aesthetics, musicology, linguistics, philosophy, and, due to the family business, mechanical engineering. Among those from whom he received important impulses for his philosophical development was Steiner, especially his early epistemological writings; Witzenmann later explored the significance of these early works for Steiner's anthroposophy.[8] It is noteworthy that between 1925 and 1928 he attended several of Husserl's lectures in Freiburg including the *Basic Problems of Logic, Nature and Spirit, Introduction to Phenomenology*, and *Phenomenological Psychology*. Although Witzenmann never explicitly referred to Husserl, these experiences must have inspired him strongly as can be seen from his use of certain Husserlian terms, which, however, he used in his own way, more or less differently from Husserl. Despite his academic efforts and due to certain biographical obstacles, not least because of his aspiration to completeness and the rejection of his anthroposophical background by his second doctoral advisor Karl Jaspers, Witzenmann's linguistic and philosophical dissertation projects failed. Subsequently, after the Second World War, he pursued activities as an editor for an anthroposophical journal (*Die Drei*) and publishing house (*Verlag Freies Geistesleben*) and wrote quite a few essays developing Steiner's approach on a philosophical level. Since that time, he held countless courses and lectures on epistemology, philosophy, art contemplation, and social aesthetics—all guided by his individual approach of structure phenomenology.

---

[8] Steiner, 1958a, 1958b, 2003

In 1951, he joined the family business as technical director and was appointed to the board of the General Anthroposophical Society in 1963. Some years later, due to an irreconcilable disagreement with the other board members, Witzenmann was excluded from the committee. Nonetheless, he unswervingly continued his research and teaching activities in numerous lectures in various contexts and published his most important work in the last decade of his life—his "Structure phenomenology" as the methodological and conceptual core.[9]

2. The Role of Introspection

The briefly sketched biographical outline illustrates some of Witzenmann's intellectual and professional background and makes his broad and experience-based approach to phenomenology understandable. In his writings, he often starts from simple conceptual considerations or everyday perceptual situations leading to fine-grained introspective or meditation-like observations of perceptual, cognitive, social, and other consciousness-related phenomena and processes. By way of the "logical organization of observations" (p. 94), Witzenmann arrives at the formulation of fundamental structures and laws continuously penetrating from the descriptive level into comprehensive epistemological and even ontological dimensions. This means that for structure phenomenology introspection as a method plays a more significant or, at least, more explicit role than for phenomenology in the Husserlian tradition. Husserl's

---

[9]For further biographical information, see Hartmann, 2010, 2013; Wagemann, 2019, 2020b.

ambivalent attitude toward introspection may have been shaped by his profound mathematical education and his critical distance to the inductive method of the empirical sciences.[10] Therefore, his own method of phenomenological reduction should serve to leave behind the idiosyncrasy and contingency of empirical-psychological data and to arrive at direct intuitive insight into essential structures of consciousness. However, as Gutland points out, intuiting such structures cannot be done without employing a certain form of introspection referring to the generalizable aspects of conscious experience.[11] For Witzenmann, concordantly, not only the person-related occasions, efforts, and actions of searching for an intuitive insight are accessible via *introspective observation*, but also its successful resonance with the qualitative coherence of this content itself. On a structural level, there are actually no introspective observations that cannot be generalized—that is, embedded into a certain conceptual context such as, for example, *thinking act* and *thought content* (p. 31). Hence, the question in each case is rather which conceptual context enables a specific observation. From the perspective of philosophy of science, this means that Witzenmann's extension of the meaning of introspection is in line with Popper's and Fleck's insight that "pure" or "apodictic" observation of facts or phenomena without any preconceived or, at least, provisional ideas is not possible.[12] Hence, eye-opening ideas or theories have to be intuited for and before any observation, even in order to make

---

[10]Pro introspection: Husserl, 1973a, p. 23; Husserl, 1977; contra introspection: Husserl, 1980, p. 38. See also Gutland, 2018; Sinha, 1969; Thomasson, 2003
[11]Breyer & Gutland, 2016; Gutland, 2018
[12]Fleck, 1979; Popper, 2002

it possible to introspectively observe the structure of intuition actually occurring in countless individual cases—if this structure is to be assigned a validity that can be generalized to all these cases. Consequently, through a rejection of all *a priori* constructs, to some of which Husserl also succumbs in his idealistic aspirations, structure phenomenology joins the paradigmatic core of modern empirical science and expands its applicability to first-person research. And, as a second implication, structure phenomenology describes a way in which pre-reflective (preconscious) intuitions and Gestalt-formations can be made introspectively conscious step by step.

Witzenmann's findings are therefore not to be understood as apodictically intuited structures, but rather as experience-based hypotheses to be further investigated. However, his approach differs from conventional empirical research as it does not aim at external measurements and object-related theories. Since his first-person observations, due to their subtle; processual; and, to an extent, even paradoxical character, defy rigid propositions subject to a bivalent logic of true and false, Witzenmann oriented himself to what Steiner called an *exceptional state* of observation distinguished by a methodological *direction of attention* or *gaze-direction* (p. 11).[13] This sounds like what Husserl later denoted as *turn of the gaze* from the things as they are initially experienced and assessed in the natural attitude (e.g., as existing in external reality) toward the analysis of their subjective appearance.[14] However, as indicated above, in order to introspectively observe valid structures of subjective experience conceptual means for

---

[13]Steiner, 1958b, 2003
[14]Husserl, 1997, p. 110

access and communication are needed; these can also be referred to as a "performative coherence" making reproducible conditions possible for such observations.[15] In this sense, linguistic expressions shall not be deemed to assert the existence of objects and their properties or the truth of conclusive argumentation, but rather serve as referential and eye-opening signposts to experiential nuances and phases of one's own mental activity and complementary phenomenal content. Whereas Wittgenstein ends his *Tractatus Logico-Philosophicus* with the words "whereof one cannot speak, thereof one must be silent," Witzenmann advocates the view that the only thing worth talking about is the unspeakable.[16] That is because language as such does not draw any boundaries but rather transcends its own realm as well as the limits of factuality and even conceptuality—and for this reason the research attitude ultimately depends only on the researcher's decision for an attributive or referential use of language.[17] With a referential use of language and concepts, it should therefore not be a problem to speak in an observational—not speculative—sense of the conceptual and non-conceptual, as Witzenmann does in the context of his investigations. In Husserl's work, by contrast, the methodological coordination of introspective experience and linguistic expression seems to be relatively underdeveloped.[18]

Against this background, Witzenmann's use of introspection can also be justified against the prevailing skepticism in contemporary psychological and philosophical consciousness research.[19] Not

---

[15] Petitmengin & Bitbol, 2013, p. 270
[16] Wittgenstein, 1999, p. 27; Witzenmann, 1984a, p. 341
[17] Donnellan, 1966; Oevermann, 2016
[18] Depraz et al., 2003; Gutland, 2018
[19] Dennett, 2018; Ryle, 2009; Schwitzgebel, 2008

only in phenomenology but also in conventional research routines introspection is inevitably and implicitly involved, for instance in the decision-making on a viable research strategy or in explaining unexpected anomalies in acquired data.[20] Just as phenomenology, as mentioned above, is a necessary though mostly implicit element of any scientific procedure, the same applies to introspection. The only difference is that, in this context, phenomenology is used to initially explore the objects of research, while introspection refers to the research-related actions and insights regarding the scientist's mental life. In experimental psychology, for example, without introspective skills the researchers could not arrive at innovative experimental designs and at tasks that they expect to be likely to produce certain effects. Here, and similarly in the philosophy of the mind, introspection and phenomenology in their implicit forms already refer to each other by virtue of the topic, but—even with the topic of consciousness—neither explicitly nor in their connection reach the level of methodological awareness. Despite the continuing reservations against introspection, various studies have shown that these do not ultimately provide criteria for a fundamental rejection of self-observation as a research method, but can be overcome by appropriate measures.[21] In this direction, a methodologically integrated combination of phenomenology and introspection, as pursued by Witzenmann's approach, can also be expected to provide new insights for a general theory of science.

---

[20] Jack & Roepstorff, 2003; Reisberg et al., 2003
[21] Danziger, 1980; Lieberman, 1979; Weger & Wagemann, 2015

3. Intentionality and the Basic Structure

Turning again to Witzenmann's relation to Husserl, a further significant case of similarity and difference can be found in the topic of *intentionality*. While Husserl, adopting and reinforcing Brentano's notion, ascribes to intentionality an overall significant role for mental life, in Witzenmann this concept only refers to one partial aspect in the constitution of conscious experience.[22] On the one hand, as will be shown, this shift in meaning makes a new understanding of Husserl's intricate concept of constitution possible.[23] On the other hand, Husserl's understanding of intentionality can also be found in Witzenmann analysis of the natural attitude, although it is not called by this term. The crucial point here is that intentionality must be comprehended with different though interrelated meanings regarding the above-mentioned levels or states of conscious experience. Intentionality, in Husserl's basic understanding of a relatedness of individual consciousness (noesis) to certain contents (noema), is well suited to explain the natural attitude of everyday consciousness as a subject-object relation. In the natural attitude, this structure remains implicit and unquestioned, in phenomenological description it must become explicit as such and then bracketed regarding the obstructive ontological belief and associated patterns of conviction. For Husserl, this is the only possible path for a methodological ascent from detached phenomenal properties through their eidetic variation to an insight into the eidetic species of the initial phenomenon. In contrast

---

[22]Husserl, 1977, 1997
[23]Zahavi, 2003

to the descriptive analysis of lived experience or the interpretation of such types of experience in certain contexts (e.g., linguistic, artistic, socio-cultural), transcendental phenomenology aims at the analysis of the general form of certain types of experience.[24] Here, as said, intentionality is mostly seen as the basic form of experience which, according to its specific type, appears in infinitely many modes (perception, judgment, hope, etc.) and with infinitely many contents (aspects of what is perceived, judged, hoped, etc.).[25]

From Witzenmann's point of view, the question arises as to how fundamental intentionality is, not only as a structure of the natural attitude, but also regarding a phenomenological investigation of its constitution. This also raises the question of the methodological basis on which a valid answer to the first question can be expected. Or to put it differently: (1) What role can intentionality, if rightly asserted for the natural attitude, also play for a phenomenologically sophisticated mode of observation? (2) Is there an intentionality toward intentionality—be it a second-order or self-referential form of intentionality—or does the knowledge of the intentional structure just result from speculative reflection on the natural attitude but not from first-person observation of its constitution? Since a detailed discussion of these questions including the ongoing debates[26] would go beyond the scope of this introduction, only one short remark can be made here before Witzenmann's proposed solution is outlined. Regarding higher-order theories of intentionality, their aim can be described in explaining phenomenal consciousness through

---

[24]Husserl, 1977, 1983
[25]Crane, 2003; Searle, 1983
[26]E.g., Dreyfus, 1982; Gurwitsch, 2010; Rosenthal, 1990

higher-order representations which are not or do not necessarily have to be phenomenally conscious as, for instance, in the distinction of phenomenal consciousness and access consciousness.[27] In contrast to Husserl's aspiration to an idealistic account of constitution, this line of thought pursues the naturalization of consciousness, because it supposedly permits the assignment of a constitutive role to neural states or processes in explaining consciousness.[28] However, even if hierarchical orders of intentional monitoring are rejected and intentionality is conceived rather as a fundamental or even self-referential aspect of experience, as in self-representational models,[29] this, in methodological regard, resides on the level of abstract and speculative argumentation—and therefore cannot explain the supposed constitutive role of intentionality on the level of a strict experience-based phenomenological method.

For Witzenmann, this distinction between different forms of consciousness makes sense since it clearly distinguishes the resultant and thus naïve state of lifeworld consciousness from the process by which it is constituted. Between these poles, however, structure phenomenology explores a way of becoming phenomenally conscious of what has not been accessed by consciousness beforehand, namely of the formative process or constitution of conscious structures. In this context, Witzenmann solves the above-mentioned problem of grounding intentionality—a problem that otherwise threatens to lead to an infinite regress of iterated intentional acts[30] or might

---

[27] Block, 1995; Carruthers, 2005
[28] E.g., Powell et al., 2010
[29] Kriegel & Williford, 2006; Smith, 2004
[30] As in Husserl, 1983, p. 174

eventually result in dropping the phenomenological method—by reducing the number of possible structures to only one *basic structure* while liberating the concept of intentionality from the burden of self-explanation, which it cannot redeem. Thus, the central finding of structure phenomenology is the basic structure—the "unification of percept and concept" (p. 5)—which is seen to be equally valid for all types of conscious experience although adaptable to various epistemic and ontic conditions. In this connection, due to its "directedness that in itself points beyond itself" (p. 38) intentionality does not play an overall substantiating role, but the role of one noetic as well as noematic activity level among others within the integrative process of structure formation. Consequently, this process and its phenomenological observation must be explained by corresponding mental activity levels between "concept" and "percept" operating above and below intentionality—but also may be interpreted as its variations—the full sequence of which reads as follows: *Actuality*, *intentionality*, *metamorphosis*, and *inherence*.

Insofar as specific content must be assigned to intentionality, it becomes understandable that in structure formation there are two types of content between which the sequence of transitional stages mediates and which, in Husserlian terminology, can be distinguished as noematic and hyletic or, in structure phenomenology, as *evidential* or *conceptual* and *non-evidential* or *non-conceptual*. According to the recasted meaning of intentionality, however, these contents and, especially, the hyletic aspect are aligned differently in structure phenomenology; this can be seen from the following three points: (1) Insofar as intentionality, also according to Witzenmann, only involves the content-wise orientation toward an object-related goal, but not necessarily its achievement, non-conceptual or hyletic phenomenality can also be denoted as an intentional content, albeit not in a noematic or attributive sense. Rather through directed attention—with, for instance, negative or paradoxical terms—the non-conceptual can be addressed as the experiential counterpart of the conceptual and hence as an equally necessary and asymmetric condition of structure. Thus, both the conceptual and the non-conceptual are to be seen as intentional "quasi-objects" transitionally occurring in the formation of what is conventionally understood as intentional objects. Since Witzenmann synonymously denotes the conceptual and non-conceptual as the evidential and non-evidential, respectively, let me add a brief reference to and demarcation from Brentano's understanding of evidence. For Brentano, evidence (German: *Evidenz*) is not something that goes to prove a belief, an assumption, an assertion, or something of that kind, but rather an experiential obviousness, particularly regarding judgments about objects of inner experience.[31] Here it becomes clear that Witzenmann's use of the term evidence differs from Brentano's in that Witzenmann also speaks about the non-evidential as a certain introspective experience which, however, cannot be stated in a judgmental way but rather only indicated by attentional direction. Erroneously transferring Brentano's notion to Witzenmann's would lead to an "evidence about the non-evident." Actually, Witzenmann restricts evidence to a sub-area of introspective experience, namely the *reciprocal determination* (p. 15) between a thinking act and a (conceptual) thought content occurring in what Husserl (and also Steiner) denotes as intuition. In

---

[31] Brentano, 1995; Meyer et al., 2018

contrast, he describes experiential contact with the non-evidential (e.g., fragmented perceptual stimuli or a logical gap in reasoning) as a *rebound* or *rejection* since it completely lacks coherence with which mental activity can only unite. (2) Witzenmann broadens the functional scope of the non-conceptual "percept" beyond Husserl's understanding of the hyletic as sensorial impression to all conscious structures which, in any sense, require conceptual processing. This justifies the generalization of the basic structure and provides for the subsumption of all phenomena under the non-conceptual or non-evidential that (at least initially) appear to be incomplete, incoherent, fragmented, or decomposed. Here, it must be noted that the non-conceptual mostly occurs as a breaking abyss between conceptually integrated matters of fact, thus marking their not yet completed coherence at one point. Against this background, even thinking activity that is being performed (noesis), before it achieves success, can be understood as the quasi-hyletic and, hence, non-conceptual counterpart of its aspired thought content (noema). Or, in other words, before achieving reciprocal determination with the evidential, a thinking act remains non-evidential for itself. (3) In contrast to the one-sided relation between the noematic and the hyletic in Husserl's conception, in Witzenmann not only is the latter structured by the former, but also the non-conceptual has a significant impact on the conceptual. This can be explained as individualizing the universal conceptual potential to a single case of appearance and extends intentionality (in the processual sense) to the further dynamic stages of metamorphosis and inherence. It is only at the stage of inherence that the conceptual side of a structure is completely adapted to its non-conceptual side (e.g., sensory stimulus, logical gap) and hence also appears as formed by the latter; for this reason Witzenmann speaks in this connection of "forming formability" (p. 39).—In sum, in the basic structure as introduced by Witzenmann, the intentional contents of "concept" and "percept" described above are brought together "in the relationship characteristic of the unification process" (p. 5). Regarding the dynamic relation between the conceptual and the non-conceptual and its experiential accessibility, far-reaching references for the McDowell-Dreyfus debate can be drawn.[32]

As a further consequence of these adjustments of phenomenological basic notions, the two-sided relation of Husserlian intentionality (noesis—noema) is broken up and extended to a threefold relation of noetic activity oscillating between the actualized noema (the evidential or universal concept), and its individualized or objectified (inherential) stage referring to what was *non-evidential* or *non-conceptual* (the hyletic side of the percept) in the epistemic process beforehand. Complementary to the actualized noema, which is experienced as evidential or *self-explanatory content*, the particular mental act can be denoted as *self-giving* due to its self-efficacy in the acquisition of the conceptual and the recomposition of the non-conceptual content which initially appears as decomposed. Hence, in Witzenmann's approach, the basic structure of consciousness is conceived as the procedural integration of structurally asymmetric yet complementary forms of intentional (conceptual and non-conceptual) content (or "quasi-objects") via characteristic stages and with the decisive contribution of individual and observable mental activity. Hence, we can distinguish various forms of intentionality

---

[32]Schear, 2013; Wagemann, 2018; Wagemann et al., 2018

and intentional content in two dimensions (Figure 1). The first dimension refers to different states or levels of conscious observation: (A1) The comparatively naïve state of the lifeworld in which object- and subject-related intentional content is experienced in the natural attitude and analyzed in application-oriented, descriptive forms of phenomenology. Since everything but intentionality itself—as an aspect of the examination—is examined here, Witzenmann calls this case *heteronomous observation* (p. 19). (A2) The (structure-) phenomenologically trained "exceptional" state in which, inter alia, intentionality itself becomes an explicit, process-related content which Witzenmann calls *autonomous observation* (p. 19). Here we enter the second dimension in which intentional content is distinguished with respect to different genetic layers and further aspects of noetic activity and noematic universality, the most significant of which are as follows: (B1) Conceptual or evidential content which is structurally constitutive for consciously experienced reality and which appears in four transitional stages (actuality, intentionality, metamorphosis, and inherence). (B2) Non-conceptual or non-evidential content

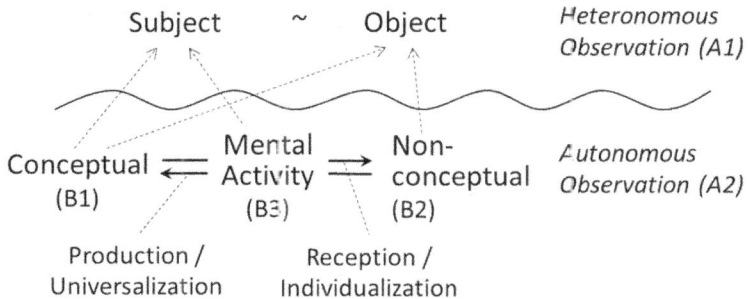

FIGURE 1 *Forms of Intentionality and Intentional Content.*

which appears as incoherent, fragmented, or decomposed and requires recomposition. (B3) Individual mental activity which accesses conceptual and non-conceptual content via corresponding microgestures (production, reception), and which initiates and co-performs the transition of the evidential toward the non-evidential. In this transition, the evidential content is individualized by the non-evidential which, in turn, is embedded into the law-like relations of the evidential and hence universalized by it. This basic process applies on the heteronomous level to both the reified object and personalized subject which emerge from specific combinations of conceptual and non-conceptual content. Hence, as mentioned above, not only sensory or intellectual stimuli but also mental activity can take the structural role of the non-conceptual which, in this case acting alone, unites with person-related attributes as conceptual contents.[33] While here, from the activity side, interesting references to the mental-action debate can be made,[34] regarding content there are promising clues in the philosophy of perception to a cross-modal "structure in which features are assigned to discrete, complex, selectively persisting individuals that are grasped as objective."[35]

Two points that clearly set Witzenmann's conception apart from others currently debated shall be highlighted once again. First, there is the extension of intentionality from a bivalent relation to a dynamic

---

[33] From a psychological perspective, the self-concept expands to a multidimensional construct including social, emotional, physical, and other aspects (Marsh & Craven, 2006). While this implies bundle theories of the self (Baumeister, 1998; Klein, 2014), structure phenomenology proves the core self in potentially self-conscious mental activity. What certainly goes in this direction, however, is Watzl's (2018) conception of the "attentional self."
[34] Fiebich & Michael, 2015; Wagemann & Raggatz, 2021; Wagemann, 2021, 2022a/b
[35] O'Callaghan, 2008, p. 826

stage in the transition between conceptuality and non-conceptuality; in other forms of phenomenology non-conceptuality often seems to remain intricate and unclear.[36] In Bernhard Waldenfels's *Phenomenology of the Alien*[37] the aspect of non-conceptuality at least plays a significant role; this leads to a recasting of intentionality as responsivity, which is challenged to bring meaning to what initially appears meaningless. However, Waldenfels does not clearly differentiate between the responsive subject (its mental activity) and the content side of the response (conceptuality) and therefore does not come to the structure-forming processes explained above.[38] More intensively than in phenomenological contexts, non-conceptuality is treated, for example, in Heinz von Foerster's second-order cybernetics ("undifferentiated encoding"),[39] in Noam Chomsky's Poverty-of-the-Stimulus argument[40] and in certain debates in analytic philosophy of mind.[41] All these accounts point to a certain extent in the direction of what structure phenomenology addresses with the notion of the (non-)conceptual or (non-)evidential—without, however, entering the field of systematic first-person observation.

The second point refers to the activity-side of intentionality which, according to the complementary intentional contents in the basic structure, consists of two different forms of phenomenal givenness. This means that insofar as the manifold modes in which intentional content is given according to Husserl's understanding

---

[36] Siewert, 2017
[37] Waldenfels, 2011
[38] Wagemann, 2010
[39] Foerster, 2003, pp. 214–15
[40] Laurence & Margolis, 2001
[41] E.g., Crane, 1992; Pylyshyn, 2009

(perception, representation, emotion, etc.) can be reduced to the basic structure as an integration of conceptual and non-conceptual content, these modes of givenness, at a constitutive level, also consist of specific combinations of corresponding mental activity. While the conceptual is given through *productive apprehension*—proceeding from the unfolding of a thinking act to its resonant unification with a thought content—the non-conceptual is given by *receptive up-take*—starting from gaze direction toward something unknown and continuing to the rebound from its alien peculiarity (p. 11). In structure phenomenology, productivity and receptivity are seen as the basic modes of mental activity; their dynamic combination makes it possible to access the complementary structural components (contents) and to co-perform their integration. It is only then that the modes of givenness specific to the type of experience to which most phenomenologists refer come about.

4. The Deposited Memory Layer

The reason why the basic structure and its dynamics are not obvious to naïve and even common phenomenological observation is that only their derivative results are manifest on the first levels of investigation. While these results suggest that things as such, or at least their descriptive properties, are finished facts, the structure-phenomenological analysis shows that all structured forms furnishing our lifeworld are made up of a certain mixture of conjunctive and disjunctive elements. Thus, objects of any kind are only the objectified end points of a process to which our own mental activity contributes in a specific way. To pave the way to this insight, Witzenmann begins this book with a critical discussion and refutation of theories that attempt to explain reality as an ontic state pre-given to human cognition; in a Husserlian sense, this can be interpreted as the bracketing of misleading beliefs about existence. Nevertheless, in the further analysis, Witzenmann arrives at a different and, to a certain extent, deeper explanation of lifeworld experience based on the structure-genetic conditions; this shall be illustrated by the following comparison with William James und Husserl. In fact, in his investigation of *pure experience* as the "primal stuff or material in the world... of which everything is composed," James distinguishes conjunctive and disjunctive qualities, which is in line with Witzenmann's understanding of the conceptual and non-conceptual.[42] However, the fact that he regards both parts as given in the same receptive way firstly implies an equality of these structurally asymmetric components of reality and, secondly, denies any preceding processuality between these elements which would be accessible to corresponding forms of mental activity (e.g., receptive, productive). In a similar way, Husserl asserts a passive, affective, and pre-given character of object-related experience prior to any epistemic dynamic.[43] A closer analysis shows that he, too, if we put it in James's terms, points to conjunctive (universal) and disjunctive (individual) aspects; however, they seem to be already merged as indicated in his seemingly paradoxical notion of a "familiar unfamiliarity" and the "universal horizon 'object' with particular indications or, rather, prescriptions."[44] As a more concrete example, Husserl's investigation

---

[42]James, 1912, p. 4
[43]Husserl, 1973b, p. 28 f.
[44]Husserl, 1973b, p. 38

of a red ball can be mentioned, which, bracketing the claim of existence of a three-dimensional sphere, only shows a plane graded in different shades of red.[45] Although this change of perspective may be unaccustomed, it does not go beyond intentionality understood as variations of the as-structure[46] and does not lead to the processual constitution of both percepts, the sphere and the plane.

From the perspective of structure phenomenology, these observations by James and Husserl can be understood as an indication that they must have been preceded by a process of mutual interaction of conjunctive (conceptual) and disjunctive (perceptual) elements, which, however, escaped their observation. As long as attention is directed to the results of this process—the objects and their properties or objectness as such and its structural features—it is as if the process does not exist at all. Consequently, the supposition of a pre-given objective presence must be regarded as a mistaken conception and can be interpreted as a reminiscence or memory of its preceding constitution. Hence, Witzenmann's analyses lead him to speak of a *memory layer* which is deposited upon the processual layer of the basic structure. Since, however, the concealment by the memory layer at the same time includes informative hints about what is concealed in the sense of its constitution, the concealed can be disclosed. In this way, Husserl's "familiar unfamiliarity"—the certainty of facing an object as something somehow existing but also strange—can be interpreted as an expression of a universalized particularity and thus as an already completed modification of the disjunctive (*perceptual*) element by the conjunctive (*conceptual*). Conversely, the "universal horizon

---

[45]Husserl, 2001, p. 83
[46]Doyon, 2016

'object' with particular indications or, rather, prescriptions" can be seen as Husserl's implicit articulation of an individualized coherence and thus as an already completed modification of the conjunctive under disjunctive influence. Overall, according to Witzenmann, the *supposition of objective presence* (p. 58) in the natural attitude and, as demonstrated, even in mainstream phenomenology proves to be a memorative reference to the structurally deeper layer of processual constitution.

Against this background, Witzenmann explains how our own (initially pre-reflective) mental activity and bodily organization are involved in the deposition of the memory layer upon the basic structure. Because mental activity enables and drives recomposition of decomposed fragments in the structural basic layer, it also participates in the mentioned modifications of the conceptual and the non-conceptual components resulting in the memory layer. As the conceptual element undergoes the transition from its actualized (universal) to its inherent (individualized) form, the moderating activity increases the ability to exert this transition and hence can better individualize the same concept in subsequent situations; this is what Witzenmann denotes as *active disposition* (p. 49). On the other hand, since one functional aspect of the sensory-neural system must be conceived as a radical decomposition (modal dequalification and neural fragmentation) of coherent lifeworld stimuli to non-conceptual relics, the complementary process of recomposition, as performed and observed on the mental side, also has to be enabled by the neural side.[47] This enabling—which is certainly not causation of

---

[47]Wagemann, 2011; Wagemann et al., 2018

phenomenal consciousness but rather a decrease of decomposition—makes it possible to overcome the critical state of the mental decomposition effect; on the neural side, this also leads to significant modifications and hence to a consistent interpretation of synaptic plasticity. Complementary to the active disposition, the potential usability of specifically shaped synaptic connectivity patterns—which due to their reference to meaning structures of the lifeworld appear as pre-universalized—is denoted as *passive disposition* by Witzenmann (p. 49).[48] In short, the subject-object relationship and thus also Husserl's understanding of passive synthesis can be understood as the result of mutual influences in the basic process, on the one hand of mental activity and conceptuality (leading to the subject-side), on the other hand of physiological conditions and conceptuality (leading to the object-side, see Figure 1).

If the subject-object relation is not the original structure of consciousness, but the derivative result of a previous process, it can be interpreted as a structural remembrance of this process. This, as Witzenmann points out, also sheds new light on the psychological topic of memory as spontaneous or deliberate recall of past events. Given the controversy between the archival or storage account[49] and the reconstructivist approach,[50] a compromise in accordance with structure phenomenology consists in considering both stored items and reconstructing mental activity.[51] In this sense, *functional*

---

[48]Later in the text, Witzenmann uses instead of the terms *active* and *passive disposition* what we have translated as *disposition of recollection* or *recollective disposition* (Erinnerungsdisposition) and *disposition of memory* or *memory disposition* (Gedächtnisdisposition).
[49]Brockmeier, 2015
[50]Robins, 2016
[51]Weger et al., 2018

remembering, which is usually presumed to contain a very first reference to something experienced earlier can be clarified as a later repetition of *structural remembering*—that is the prior deposited memory layer—which was established at the moment of the current experience and led to a subject-object relation. Therefore, Witzenmann explains the general possibility of remembering past experiences by the same mental ("active") and bodily ("passive") dispositions that are acquired during participation in the basic structure. In this light, the conventional approaches to memory may converge in respect of the finding that the "stored items" contain neither any potentially conscious content nor its representation in themselves but rather provide "the universally predisposed traces" which are taken up by our "individually predisposed conceptual activity" (p. 53).

Taking into account that memories generally have a more attenuated, indistinct, and incomplete character compared with the original experiences, it becomes clear that our normal consciousness, which, according to Witzenmann, also turns out to be memory-like, only contains a pale reflection or representation of the procedural reality of the basic structure. Particularly regarding the topic of perception, this concept of superimposed structural layers with different proximity to reality constitution can be related to the debate between representationalist and anti-representationalist accounts.[52] Like the above discussion, the point is not to assume one of these two positions, but rather to show to what extent both seem to be partly right and partly inadequate in the context of structure phenomenology. What must in any case be critically rejected

---

[52]Nanay, 2015

regarding both approaches is the often tacitly presupposed reference of the perceiving individual to objects that are ready given as such and preformed in some way. In contrast, however, it makes sense to speak of representations in relation to perceived objects insofar as the process of structure formation in the memory layer has arrived at a first result. Then representations as individualized (inherent) conceptuality, comprising a hierarchical complex of interrelated coherences which is fixed to a single case (e.g., the currently seen maple tree in front of my house), make it possible to refer to the non-conceptual content of sensory perception and thus actually extend in manifold ways into perceived reality.[53] Obviously, this does not necessarily mean that perceptual representations are static and abstract entities, as anti-representationalists critically note, but rather something that constitutes only one part, namely the conceptual side, of a perceived structure. The whole structure, of course, can only be adequately conceived when its other part, the perceptual field or environment and, moreover, the related interaction of the perceiving subject, are also considered, as enactivists emphasize. Indeed, this refers to the processuality of the basic structure, but neglects, as for example in the context of the Gestalt circle oscillating between perception and movement[54] the necessity of meaningful coherences (conceptuality)—without which nothing at all can be perceived in the confrontation with non-conceptual stimuli. Here again, controversial approaches can be reconciled by demonstrating their relevance to partial aspects of the basic structure and its superimposed layers.

---

[53]Steiner, 1958b
[54]Freeman, 1999; Weizsäcker, 1986

5. Reality Access and Ontological Stratification

A fourth key topic of structure phenomenology to be considered in this introduction revolves around being and reality and hence addresses the nexus between phenomenology and ontology. Although these topics may not initially seem to be associated with each other,[55] Husserl, and some of his successors (e.g., Heidegger) have also touched this topic, and even in analytic philosophy, which has recently reapproached metaphysics, there seems to be an openness to experience-based accounts and phenomenological perspectives.[56] Besides this, however, "the vast majority of contemporary metaphysicians [..] is trying to do metaphysics without a distinctive source of data beyond common sense and third-person observation"[57]—and thus limits itself to the substantiation and refutation of linguistic propositions about physical matter and consciousness, which comes close to a nominalist attitude regarding concepts. Thus, concepts are used argumentatively according to abstract definitions based on properties but are not examined with view to their constitutive role for reality and consciousness, the latter of which is tacitly confined to the common sense. That common sense or the natural attitude thus deprives itself of the possibility of exploring and understanding its own grounds in the transition to methodologically guided first-person observation has already been elucidated in the previous sections.

---

[55]Sinha, 1969
[56]Dainton, 2008; Goff, 2017; Soteriou, 2013; Watzl, 2017
[57]Goff, 2017, p. 265

Here it is necessary to outline Witzenmann's concept of universals as conceptual constituents of reality to the extent that it is relevant for an understanding of this book.[58] In the context of the basic structure as the integration of concept and percept, conceptuality is restricted neither to linguistic propositions nor to the common sense level of consciousness, but rather simply stands for any coherent quality, structure, regularity, and meaning in experiential phenomena, be it in sensorial qualia, perception, emotion, imagination, or thought, for example. Understood this way, concepts are neither subject- nor object-related representations, even if they make them possible. With this extension complementary to the above conception of the non-conceptual, conceptuality possess the full range of universal potentiality that is individualized to single cases of appearance in structure formation. Since, as a central result of structure-phenomenological inquiry, mental activity is involved not only in the actualization of conceptual content that may match but also in its transition toward inherence, whereby the specific resonance of the conceptual with the non-conceptual (e.g., perceptual) can also be monitored. While, according to Witzenmann, in every formation of structure all four transitional stages (actuality, intentionality, metamorphosis, inherence) necessarily occur—this is the epistemological aspect—its ontic status and ascription to a specific region or layer of reality is determined by the completeness of stages accepted by and incorporated into the emerging structure. The difference between an inorganic and an organic structure, for example, can be clarified through the observation whether the stimulus-related dynamic of

---

[58]Further reading in German: Witzenmann, 1994

change and adaptation (metamorphosis) is only part of the conceptual and mentally active (subject-) side of the realization or also belongs to the perceptual (object-) side of the structure as an individualized feature of its own function and existence. In the first case, we are faced with an inorganic structure, in the second with an organic structure. Even if this differentiation of ontic layers is admittedly to be seen as an outcome of advanced observational expertise, it points to an immanent and non-speculative approach that in a phenomenological way connects epistemological and ontological aspects. In a sense, Itay Shani's "esonectic-exonectic divide" resembles the experiential criterion of assigning integral features either to the epistemic outside of an entity (exonectic) or to its ontic inside (esonectic).[59] Furthermore, a stratification of reality is supported by other accounts pointing to the irreducibility of each layer in relation to other layers while explaining their interconnectedness through laws of separation and integration.[60]

Fundamental to reality, in Witzenmann's view, are not hypothetical particles or elements of which things are composed, but rather constitutive wholes—concepts—and their gradual shadowing and constriction to single, "particle-like" cases that, in connection with perceptual stimuli, we habitually call objects. The fact that a certain object—for example, an apple—has further properties beyond just being an apple (e.g., color, size, taste), which are observed in a certain place and at a certain time, means that further concepts immanently connected with the apple-concept through their law-like content have also entered the realization process and built up a structure in

---

[59] Shani, 2015, p. 420
[60] Feibleman, 1954; Hartmann, 1964; for review, see Kleineberg, 2017

resonance with the non-conceptual content of the apple-stimuli. In this context, physical micro-particles appear as theoretical abstractions from the scientist's pre-reflective experience of being confronted with individual objects and beings.[61] The fact that efficient technology can be constructed based on corresponding physical models should therefore not be regarded as an implicit verification of such models. Rather, this shows that concepts are suited in a highly differentiated way to bring perceptual stimuli (e.g., related to displays of measuring devices) into comprehensible contexts that also extend to material effectiveness. However, the categorical nature of matter, that is, the sense in which it exists or does not exist, remains unaffected. The assumption that imperceptible atoms and their sub-particles exist in a similar way to a perceptible apple or even in a more fundamental way is rectified by the structure-phenomenological finding that objects of all kinds "are basic structures [unifications of concepts and percepts, J.W.] already veiled by a superficial layer" (p. 78). Thus, the most crucial point in the ontological implications of structure phenomenology is that at a fundamental level existence and reality are accessible to the human being through advanced first-person observation penetrating through the memory veil and witnessing the basic structure in which it constitutively participates. This leads, as explained, to the other important aspect that reality unfolds as a layered process based on universal coherence, which in its stratification also establishes our common-sense understanding of inorganic matter, living organisms, sentient animals, and (potentially) self-aware humans.

---

[61]Steiner, 1975. See also Schopenhauer's (1907) principle of objectification of the will and Maine de Biran's (1766–1824) idea that our understanding of persisting objects is derived from the experience of our mental will, which proceeds from a persisting self (Hallie, 1959, p. 74).

But does then, according to structure phenomenology, matter, or anything else exist in a way independent of consciousness? If not, this view would have strong idealistic traits—not least because of its emphasis on universal realism—and perhaps even a proximity to Berkeley's idealism, in which fundamental reality is completely immaterial. If yes, how could what is independent of consciousness be conceived without falling back into the speculative and transcendence-loaded habits of contemporary philosophy and physics? This question is not really clarified in Witzenmann's book but shall be briefly discussed here with reference to other texts by him and initially contextualized regarding current approaches. A first hint is Witzenmann's radical conception of the non-conceptual elements "which are all that remain of reality after the decomposition brought about by our organization" (p. 49). Thus, he obviously indicates a "reality" before decomposition which, however, must not be confused with what results from recomposition whose object- or subject-like end points may be erroneously seen to be fundamental for reality. Rather, as Witzenmann elucidates in his book *Sinn und Sein* (Sense and being, 1989a), the pre-decomposed und thus pre-known can only be understood as a necessary condition—again not causation—for human knowing which enables decomposition and recomposition as complementary processes. While decomposition can be functionally assigned to the physiological level and thus initially works independently of consciousness, concrete effects of decomposition occur at the mental level and are recomposed in a variety of ways (e.g., culture-specific, person-related) or, in the absence of interest or capability, not at all. Likewise, the possibility of experimentally combining conceptual and non-conceptual elements and monitoring success or failure of such attempts at unification indicates that there certainly is a world beyond individual consciousness.[62]

Instead of misunderstanding the pre-decomposed world, however, as material or property-related existence, for instance as "inscrutables" pre-fixed for human recognition,[63] it must be recognized as that which provides the conditions which confront human consciousness with the task and possibility of its own developmental construction in the face of decomposition. For every recomposition of the decomposed at the same time enables an original composition of the recomposing individual herself and even more so when the individual becomes aware of this process. What, according to Witzenmann, grants these conditions can be thought of as a "universal ideational coherence" (p. 32) or "super-temporal processuality" (p. 68), which outlines a fundamental, holistic, and intrinsically dynamic layer of reality from which temporal processes in two dimensions emerge.[64] The first dimension of temporality refers to cosmogenesis and natural evolution as a general, stratified horizon in which the second dimension takes place as an increasingly individualizing human development with the option to reintegrate itself into the universal context. This can be outlined as follows:[65] In cosmogenesis, matter is derived from ideational coherence through an initial deprivation or decomposition that, from the physical side, can be easily associated with the "big bang." This seems to be a consistent way of explaining why mental

---

[62]See, e.g., Wagemann, 2018
[63]Montero, 2010
[64]"The nature of things generally, in abstracto, can be specified outside of time .... It [the universe, J.W.] must be, so to speak, temporally indeterminate at the edges" (Mathews, 2011, p. 152).
[65]See Steiner, 1972; Witzenmann, 1986, 1989b

and material levels of reality appear categorically different—due to decomposition—and at the same time have an effective and lawful relationship to each other—due to their common origin. The reverse hypothesis is not logically consistent because, as has become clear, no process can be conceived which could give rise to a composition of higher levels based on lower levels without requiring hidden recourse to the higher ones[66] or leading to causal overdetermination.[67] After the initial split, evolution consists in gradually pervading matter again with ideational coherence or, in other words, in a macro-level recomposition leading to different layers of reality or regions of being—which can be understood as the essential meaning of their co-evolution. Each of the ontic layers integrates and individualizes ideational coherence in a characteristic way and therefore provides varying degrees of independence from the natural environment. The organization of the human body achieves a maximum of independence from natural determination; this appears as the mental decomposition effect of the sensory-nervous system on its bearer and as the potential freedom to individually build up reality in knowing and acting.[68] Here, in a certain sense, cosmogenesis and evolution are repeated on an individual micro-level in that they catapult the human being back again to the initial conditions of all emergence and enable it to individually recompose the decomposed stimuli—the smaller und larger crises in life—with the participation of its own mental activity. In this way, the individually conscious human makes herself

---

[66]Bennett & Hacker, 2003
[67]Kim, 2006
[68]From an anthropological perspective, decomposition salient in humans can be associated with the concept of "defective creature" coined by J. G. Herder (2002) and A. Gehlen (1988).

the carrier of cultural evolution and can reconnect with his universal origin by becoming aware of this participation.

This far-reaching conception, obviously going beyond current debates in philosophy, also indicates the spiritual or even religious dimension of structure phenomenology, which Witzenmann cautiously suggests, especially in the final chapters. Moreover, it shows that structure phenomenology certainly does have distinctive idealistic implications which, however, due to its processual, experiential, and methodological features, must not be equated with conventional forms of idealism. While the aspects of ideational coherence as the starting point for reality and the dialectical principle of decomposition and recomposition as the root for individuality are most likely to be associated with Hegel, Witzenmann criticizes his renunciation of systematic first-person observation, which in the nineteenth century can rather be found in Goethe, Maine de Biran, and Steiner.[69] Furthermore, Husserl's late idealism purports to be grounded in phenomenology; however, the experiential method of phenomenology, as mentioned, has been replaced by transcendental reflection and speculation and is thus no longer relevant for an integrated science. Apart from this general methodological distinction of structure phenomenology from other philosophical (not only idealistic) approaches, some of these nevertheless support partial aspects of its metaphysical implications. However, it follows from the preceding reflections that physicalism, Russellian monism and recent forms of compositional (atomistic) panpsychism can already be ruled out due to their belief in the constitutive priority

---

[69]Witzenmann, 2005

of parts over wholes. An approach which acknowledges the priority of wholes over parts can be found in priority monism as it considers the heterogeneous aspects of reality as "dependent fragments of an integrated whole."[70] Schaffer's identification of the whole with the cosmos would be compatible with Witzenmann's view of a super-conceptual totality fundamental for everything in the cosmos if he did not limit himself to the material cosmos. For to speak of the cosmos as a whole, even in a material sense, is not possible without having an integrative concept of the cosmos, which itself is not material, but first ensures what one is talking about at all. In this respect, a material cosmos initially conceived as the most comprehensive whole cannot be complete.

What is lacking in an exclusively material view of the cosmos can be found, for example, in Tim Crane's person-related concept of mental substances. The claim that "a mental substance is a continuant whose underlying natural principle... is mental" includes the two aspects of super-temporality (continuant) and coherence (principle) in Witzenmann's characterization of the original potential of structure.[71] While Crane focuses his consideration on the dimension of human individualization, the broader aspects of universal foundation and processuality seem to be present in Yujin Nagasawa's priority cosmopsychism. For Nagasawa, the cosmos as a whole is basically conscious and ontologically prior to individual consciousness which is instantiated by cosmic consciousness.[72] In his conception, however, it remains unclear how individual consciousness is to be derived

---

[70]Schaffer, 2010, p. 33
[71]Crane, 2004, p. 246
[72]Nagasawa & Wager, 2017; see also Shani, 2015

from cosmic consciousness—the decomposition problem. In any case, if the cosmos is originally mental and holistic, a derivation from it cannot be conceived as a mechanical division as with spatially extended, material objects since this would contradict its non-spatial and non-temporal character. Moreover, in Nagasawa's top-down view, instantiation seem to suggest that individual phenomenal consciousness is completely determined by cosmic consciousness; however, this contradicts the general loss of natural determination in humans effected by decomposition.[73] Hence, only a combination of cosmic top-down derivation with bottom-up processes relying on individual mental agents (or "substances") can lead to a consistent explanation according to Witzenmann. Instead of somehow smuggling heterogeneity into a unified whole—which is then no longer unified—as Nagasawa seems to attempt, heterogeneity can rather be understood as the outcome of the whole's own partial self-negation (decomposition); this results in something detached from its origin which possesses the necessity and possibility of reintegration. This solution of the individuation problem in panpsychism seems to be outlined by Freya Mathews with her psychoanalytic analogy of the initial "split off" from a universal consciousness leading to "autonomous complexes" of psychophysical energy to be integrated again.[74] What makes Witzenmann's metaphysical concept attractive in this respect is the fact that he finds precisely these structural-processual interrelationships at the level of individual first-person observation, at which they seem to be repeated as an expression of

---

[73]Wagemann, 2010
[74]Mathews, 2011, p. 148

their original self-referentiality. Thus, the ontological implication inherent to this book could best be termed as de-/recompositional or structure-phenomenological cosmopsychism.

6. Critical Remarks

After having outlined some of the most important aspects of structure phenomenology and its high relevance for various debates some critical remarks on Witzenmann's book shall be added. The first is related to the fact already mentioned above that Witzenmann has omitted most references of other approaches in the text. This applies not only to the approaches he critically examines, but especially to the one he considers the main reference point of his structure phenomenology, namely Steiner's. Although Witzenmann repeatedly refers to Steiner in his foreword, introduction, and some other places in the text—albeit in a more general way—the relationship of both accounts remains quite implicit. Scholars acquainted with Steiner's epistemological work will certainly have no difficulty in identifying these traces in Witzenmann's text, and there are even some articles in which Witzenmann refers explicitly and page by page to Steiner's works.[75] Of course, it is regrettable that Witzenmann did not also follow this approach in his structure phenomenology; the reasons can only be speculated about. On the one hand, perhaps he did not want to draw the reader's attention too much to Steiner to avoid negative prejudices and to present his approach to the academic reader in the

---

[75] E.g., Steiner, 1958b, 2003; Witzenmann, 1977

most neutral way possible. On the other hand, he wrote the book at an advanced age and perhaps no longer had the perseverance for meticulous referencing. Apart from this, an overview of Witzenmann's oeuvre shows that he took up and developed Steiner's work throughout consistently, with methodical rigor and in his own language.[76] Even more, with the basic structure Witzenmann identified the main thread running through most of Steiner's works and therefore provided a key for their pending philosophical and empirical analysis. However, there are also aspects of structure phenomenology that are found in Steiner's work only to some extent or not at all, so one cannot say that Witzenmann simply repeated Steiner's views. While the emergence of passive and active dispositions in individuals' ongoing participation in the basic structure is alluded, for example, in Steiner's *Theosophy*,[77] the reciprocal relation between the processual layer of the basic structure and the deposited memory layer does not seem to be thematized at all in Steiner. Nor does Steiner provide Witzenmann's clarification of the relationships between temporality and super-/subtemporality as well as between memory representation and processual presence, at least not with this analytic transparency. A brief compilation of the most important references and distinctions between Steiner's epistemology and Witzenmann's structure phenomenology would certainly have been helpful for a conceptional and historical classification of the latter. However, a comprehensive comparison of Witzenmann's approach with Steiner would go beyond the scope of this introduction and hence remains one of the research desiderata of the future.

---

[76]Wagemann, 2019, 2020b
[77]Steiner, 1987

Another question besides the sparse contextualization of structure phenomenology in Steiner's framework concerns Witzenmann's method. He introduces the structure-phenomenological method as introspective-meditative or meditation-like observation referring to what Steiner literally called *observation of the soul* ("seelische Beobachtung"),[78] but which is not explained as thoroughly as would be expected in a work with philosophical basic claim. While we have already shed some light on the role of introspection in Witzenmann's approach in philosophical terms above, the aspect of meditation and especially the relationship between the two needs further clarification since this is not enough elaborated in the book. At least, Witzenmann makes clear that an observational access to the processual layer of the basic structure cannot be achieved in the natural attitude but rather requires an exceptional state of consciousness. Accordingly, it must be assumed that his statements about the basic structure and related topics such as the memory layer, for example, cannot emerge from naïve introspection like statements about everyday feelings and thoughts but must be founded on highly trained introspective expertise. This probably entails a combination of advanced self-reflexive and metacognitive skills with an orientation toward a holistic and processual form of experience in which the individual observations are ordered and integrated.[79] Such a progression would allow to distinguish naïve and trained forms of introspection, on the one hand, and meditation as building on trained introspection as a necessary but not sufficient condition, on the other. Differently put,

---

[78]Steiner, 1958b
[79]See Advice for the Reader (Point 3).

we could perhaps speak of structure-phenomenological meditation as a kind of "second order mindfulness" insofar as it is not only about giving undivided attention to arbitrary phenomena or activities but also including attention itself as a mental activity into the scope of observation. In the book, however, there is a lack of elucidation as to how this type of observation can be exercised concretely and in which steps it can be learned and trained. In which situations, for instance, an observational differentiation of concept and percept or of thinking act and thought content can succeed is partly illustrated with examples (e.g., tree), but not systematically developed under consideration of different conditions and possible experimental tasks. Here, too, reference can be made to other texts by Witzenmann, in which he deals with meditation in more detail,[80] although this too would not yet meet the requirements of an experimental-empirical approach, at least not without further adjustments. Since Witzenmann still saw himself more as an individual researcher, an implementation of methodological quality criteria (explicit description of training conditions, person-independence, replicability, etc.), as is usual today in empirical settings, is not yet found with him. To be fair, however, it must be said that this appears comprehensible from the perspective of a more philosophical (rather than psychological-empirical) self-understanding and is also prevalent among many contemporary philosophers. A systematic exploration of Witzenmann's work through empirical first-person research has only been pursued for a few years as will be explained in the next section.

---

[80] E.g., Witzenmann, 1989c

A third point of critique refers to Witzenmann's way of presenting his approach. In the editorial foreword, Witzenmann's writing style has been characterized as sober and scientific, on the one hand, and as challenging and laborious on the other hand. However, some scholars who gave feedback on the text found it much more negative, partly in the sense of an unnecessary density and partly even as idiosyncratic and turgid. This seems to confirm the cliché sometimes circulated about continental philosophers that they deliberately complicate their texts to lend their ideas the nimbus of the mysterious, unfathomable. One can of course criticize that Witzenmann did not make it easier for his readers to understand structure phenomenology, and as one can see from his own foreword, he was not only aware of those obstacles, but even seems to have intended it that way. However, that Witzenmann finally summarizes the content of the book as a take-away message (*Advice for the Reader*) speaks more for the fact that it was not his intention to artificially obscure his presentation. After all, he leaves it up to his readers to decide whether they want to read the brief overview or the full text first. It can therefore be assumed that his intention was not to condemn readers to unnecessary wrestling with the text, but to decide how much mental effort, especially in the sense of an experimental-observational attitude, they would be willing to invest in dealing with the subject. Since he was primarily concerned with the mental activity and its training which he expected from his readers, it is debatable whether this would only be achieved with this demanding or also with a simpler form of linguistic expression. Even though Witzenmann's style is certainly not free of tendencies toward the complex continental way of writing, the text seems easier to read than some of Kant or Heidegger's, and even these authors have been studied diligently despite a difficult access. In the end, it is probably also a question of the readers' stylistic preference whereby in a philosophical context it should be ultimately thought and observation that counts more than style. And those who penetrate through the sometimes-unwieldy language to the core ideas and experiences of structure phenomenology may be motivated to reflect, criticize, and possibly develop them in their own—perhaps simpler—style.

7. Reception and Further Development of Witzenmann's Structure Phenomenology

As mentioned above, Witzenmann's work is up to now practically unknown, both in the German-speaking area and worldwide. His structure phenomenology should not be hastily associated with other similar sounding approaches such as Heinrich Rombach's structural ontology,[81] Steven R. Brown's structural phenomenology[82] or what S. Aurora and P. Flack understand under this term.[83] Remarkably, these authors make no reference to each other, let alone to Witzenmann. Nevertheless, there are some isolated links to his work in academic contexts, especially from some of his former students who referred to structure phenomenology in their dissertations or

---

[81] Rombach, 1971
[82] Brown, 2005
[83] Aurora & Flack, 2018

other contexts[84] or from other scholars.[85] A more comprehensive contextualization, application, and extension of Witzenmann's structure phenomenology is available in the editor's own doctoral thesis about the mind-brain problem and subsequent work.[86] Together with colleagues, he has published on the methodological challenges and opportunities of first-person research in psychology[87] and conducted several introspective studies on psychological topics such as *the self*,[88] *memory*,[89] *mind-wandering*,[90] and *awe and wonder*.[91] In all these studies, in addition to an initial recast of first-person methodology, specific aspects of Witzenmann's structure phenomenology are referenced and innovatively applied not only to open the field of first-person experience, but also to place it in a conceptual context that can supplement the prevailing constructs and theories in third-person research. Two further paths of this research are leading to an implementation of structure phenomenology in educational contexts, particularly in the anthropological foundations of Waldorf pedagogy,[92] on the one hand, and to empirical-introspective investigations on the experiential, processual, and agentive nature of consciousness, on the other. Building on his own introspective exploration of perceptual reversals in lifeworld situations, Wagemann developed a four-phase hypothesis of mental action which substantiates and differentiates the basic structure

---

[84]Ross, 1995; Schieren, 1998; Veiga, 2016
[85]Wettig, 2009
[86]Wagemann, 2010, 2011
[87]Weger & Wagemann, 2015a, 2015b
[88]Weger et al., 2016
[89]Weger et al., 2018a
[90]Weger et al., 2018b
[91]Weger & Wagemann, 2018
[92]Wagemann, 2016, 2017

according to Witzenmann.[93] This hypothesis has already been tested, strengthened, and partly extended in empirical studies.[94] The mentioned extension concerns the dimension of emotional experience or metacognitive feelings associated with mental activity, as examined in the two latter studies, and a cross-modal replication of this activity pattern for vision and audition.[95] This, for example, builds bridges to the psychological topics of self-efficacy and problem-solving and to the philosophical debates on cognitive phenomenology and mental action. The findings demonstrate that even untrained testpersons can respond to the question as to what it is like to experience and control specific forms of mental activity that they themselves perform. Further studies on mental activity in nonverbal social interaction[96] and directed thinking[97] confirm the validity of the basic structure in different cognitive fields. However, it is only possible to arrive at such generalizable results by orienting toward accepted research criteria such as reproducible experimental conditions, well-defined tasks, samples of independent participants, systematic data analysis (qualitative and quantitative), and hypothesis-driven theory building—which all must be adapted to first-person research. One important point in this context is the fine-tuned demand characteristic in introspective experiments, as it challenges the participants to neatly observe and control their mental activity and emotional states while trying to accomplish the task, which is nothing else than consciously building up the basic structure

---

[93] Wagemann, 2018
[94] Wagemann et al., 2018; Wagemann, 2020a; Wagemann & Raggatz, 2021
[95] Wagemann, 2022b
[96] Wagemann & Weger, 2021
[97] Wagemann, 2022a

under controlled conditions. Among other aspects and research strategies, this seems to be one possibility to take up Witzenmann's legacy of structure phenomenology and make it usable for future research. Hence, it is to be hoped that the field of research staked out in this book will be systematically opened by more researchers and further expanded as well as refined.

STRUCTURE PHENOMENOLOGY

FOREWORD

This study[98] is intended to serve as a brief outline of a methodical investigation of an extended field of research. It pursues three intentions:

i   Firstly, it attempts to show that contemporary consciousness, if unaltered by training, is a representational consciousness. This consciousness obscures our participation in true reality, though not to such an extent that it remains inaccessible. This presumption of inaccessibility adopts an interpretation of consciousness in terms of an affection theory of perception, which emerged from the natural sciences. In contrast, structure phenomenology advocates the human capacity to apprehend reality. The human being exercises this capacity in a fundamental process of wakeful existence continuously and in a manner that is, for the most part, subconscious, yet can nevertheless be made conscious. The layer of representation superimposed on this basic process is a metamorphosis of the formative powers active in its own emergence. One result of structure phenomenology is that our usual form of consciousness, which is merely derived from our contact with reality and thus lacks unmediated reality, nevertheless provides clear evidence of our capacity to apprehend reality.

---

[98]This is an amended and extended revision of the article of the same title [Witzenmann, 1983b].

The author regards this as an important result in regard to the requirements of a modern inner attitude.

ii Secondly, this study aims to show that a scientific mindset in the modern sense, which observes the connection of concepts with the contents of observation, passes over into a modern, scientifically oriented form of meditation.

iii Lastly, this study attempts to explain the role universals play in the construction of reality and in human contact with reality. A more detailed elucidation of the organic relation between the evidence of universals and the possibility for their actualization, intentionality, and metamorphosis, will be left for a further study, as will an explication of their double generality with respect to subjective human acts and generalizable objects in which they become fixed.

The final section provides advice for the reader. This may be desirable because the following presentation expects the reader to abandon his or her usual mindset. This summary appears, however, at the end because the author believes that the altered state of consciousness he wishes to impart will be most strikingly and effectively won when the reader, without prior facilitation, partakes of the same efforts which the author himself underwent to arrive at these results. Becoming acquainted with their reward afterward leads to a greater familiarity with them. However, it is left to the discretion of the readers to decide for themselves how best to approach this text.

Herbert Witzenmann
Dornach, Switzerland, August 1983

Introduction: Demarcation and Structure

Within the field of research stemming from Rudolf Steiner's epistemological ontology, structure phenomenology, which has only been recently developed and is still relatively neglected, deserves its due attention. Not only because it has already obtained noteworthy results[1] and has opened up an unusually rich field of research, but

---

This treatise is a reproduction of the contents of Lectures given at the universities of Bochum and Münster. The objection could be raised against this presentation that it makes an uncritical premature decision on actual infinity (in the sense of Cantor's hierarchy of infinities). The author will address this unfounded objection at length in a forthcoming work on the problem of universals [Unfortunately, this work was not realized.]. This problem has recently attracted significant attention from researchers in the United States (such as Ramsey [1925], Quine [1981], and Goodman [1956]). However, the unprejudiced reader may notice that the problem of universals is sufficiently considered here with the depth demanded in this context. At the same time the problem is presented in a way that makes aspects manifest that so far have not sufficiently been considered in research or not even been recognized at all.

[1]Topics such as the structure of truth (the experimental judgments, [Witzenmann, 1978]), the linguistic structure (the "ego-morphosis," [Witzenmann, 1978]), the aesthetic structure (the morphological counterflow, [Witzenmann, 1985]), and the legal structure (regulative and constitutive legal systems, [Witzenmann, 1984b]) could be developed. In addition, numerous spiritual-scientific structural analyses could be undertaken.

also because the difficulties and consequences of the problem of generation (which is one of the most intractable of epistemological problems) become apparent with particular forcefulness. Therefore, a concentrated synopsis of this newly developed area will be given in the following pages. An analysis of the affinities and dissimilarities of the proposed treatment with other branches of science that have recently become well known will be left out of this account as it would initiate lengthy discussion. Therefore, what follows does not take into consideration the structural psychology connected with Dilthey, Gestalt psychology, the structuralism influenced by de Saussure, and the epistemological structuralism represented predominantly by English-speaking researchers and with which, in the German-speaking countries, researchers such as Stegmüller are associated.

Structure phenomenology, which shall be addressed here, proceeds from an analysis of the epistemic process that is based on introspective observation and whose procedure is that of science in the true sense of the term (i.e., it is neither deductive, nor inductive; rather it is indicative in the sense of determining what is observable). Such an analysis was first given by Rudolf Steiner in his epistemological writing in connection with Goethe's doctrine of metamorphosis. Also, the relation between structure phenomenology and Goethe's morphology cannot be discussed here due to the extent of such an undertaking.[2]

---

[2] An essay on this topic by the author will be published soon [Witzenmann, 1987].

After rejecting spurious assumption, the following discussion shows the starting point of structure phenomenclogy in the *basic structure*. Then the *crucial difficulty* for the scientific procedure that arises from the basic structure shall be characterized. Finally, the *proposed solution* shall be presented, and an overview of the structure phenomenological method and its scope shall be derived from it.

1

The Basic Structure

1.1 Mistaken Conceptions of the Relation between Consciousness and Object

The basic structure can be detected in all phenomena insofar as we become conscious of them. It results from the unification of percept and concept in the relationship characteristic of the unification process. Before unfolding the basic structure in connection with Rudolf Steiner's epistemological investigations, a better understanding of it may be gained by investigating conceptions of reality and human being-in-the-world that differ from a grasp of the basic structure that is free from presuppositions.

> **a** *Sensory Affection Theory*: One of the beliefs impeding an understanding of the conditions for structure, a belief that is still widely held, is the conception of the origin of the content of consciousness according to the stimulus-receptor model.[1] In this conception our percepts are simply stimulation

---

[1] [Skinner, 1957, 1974]

states of our organism caused by imperceptible stimuli. They are therefore not objectively given entities, but rather modifications that we perceive in ourselves. Compared to the primary affections, all other contents of consciousness are secondary and therefore even further removed from the object. Whether we conceive of the extra-conscious realm in corpuscular terms or in terms of a differentiated field of quantum-statistical singularities is insignificant to the basic conception. The sensory affection theory, even if correct, cannot contribute to an understanding of the manifold construction of stationary and moving forms. Moreover, it is apt to hinder serious consideration of the conception being argued for here. Therefore, at this juncture it is necessary to draw attention to this error inasmuch as it is only possible to form judgments of the presupposed imperceptible realm using criteria found in or inferred from the realm of the perceptible. In arguing this way, the perceptible is explained by appealing to a process presupposed to be inexplicable; for it is only possible to make statements about the imperceptible that are themselves already contents of consciousness. With regard to the theory, they thus presuppose what they are supposed to explain but, with regard to this presupposition, cannot explain. Hence, the sensory affection theory presupposes that either its presuppositions or its results are false. Further, objective percepts can only be subjectified (conceived of as affections) when the subjective percepts of the human organism are objectified (though not as affections but as an objective, causal system).

b *Resemblance Theory*: In the previously characterized theory, reality is an outcome of an inference that is inadmissible according to its own presuppositions. It makes the mistake of transferring the relationship between objects and the subjective human organization to an imperceptible realm a realm that is erroneously objectified. According to another conception reality is more accessible to human experience, though still qualitatively and quantitatively far beyond the limits of observation.[2] In relation to the reality that is presupposed our percepts would then be more or less exact or more or less complete. They would therefore be capable of and require continual clarification and completion. They would thus stand in a relationship of approximation or similarity to a reality that is not fully accessible. As is the case with the illusionist conception, this is inferred, though not hypothetically, but rather by analogy. By assuming an approximation to something unknown, this conception presupposes what it purports to explain. Hence, conjectures of approximation can proliferate in the direction of lesser as well as greater similarity. Thus, the similarity hypothesis does not deliver what it purports to give, namely criteria for the human capacity for reality. Rather, it presents starting points for potentially successful measures. However, these approaches and their outcomes lie in a presupposed reality, while the human contact with reality remains unexplained and is instead replaced by anticipated objectives. Moreover,

---

[2][Bhaskar, 2008; Popper, 1963]

even if this conception were admissible, it would not be able to contribute to an understanding of the structure of worldly phenomena.

c *Homogeneity Theory*: This conception comes closer to the problem of structure insofar as it regards particulars and coherences as elements of reality that belong together. Even when modern physics makes singularities and fields merge, particulars still appear in theory due to certain relations.[3] This basic conception seems not to be in need of much discussion, but it does require a great deal of explanation. In our context it is of utmost relevance that, with respect to human cognition, this type of conception regards particulars and coherences as fundamentally equal components of reality. It does this in so far as it attributes equal pre-givenness to particulars and coherences for human cognition.[4] Being pre-given, they are fundamentally distinct in equal measure from human intentionality and thinking activity. Accordingly, the realm of human intentionality and activity stands only in a relationship of reaction or representation to objective reality. Therefore, the assumption of equal pre-givenness leads to one of the two previously mentioned conceptions that the real world is inaccessible or only partially accessible. The homogeneity theory is *the* decisive characteristic feature of a materialistic world-view (even when not recognized as such). Although it regards the realm of human intentionality and primary

---

[3] [As in the wave-particle duality or in the quantum field theory]
[4] [Shapere, 1982]

activity as the result of material processes, and thus as real, with respect to content, however, it does not regard this realm as reality-related. Therefore, in this conception reality takes on a mode of being that is alien to how we understand ourselves. The human being is not epistemically capable of apprehending reality, but rather capable of success owing to assumptions based not on reality but rather on rules of behavior.

Other spurious conceptions shall be addressed below. Because it is based on a presuppositionless analysis, Rudolf Steiner's epistemology leads to a different determination of the basic structure.

1.2 The Basic Structure in the Light of Rudolf Steiner's Epistemology

A determination of the basic structure that is free from presuppositions begins with the apprehension of a coherence and the elements to which it relates. This results in an orientation decidedly different from that of the homogeneity theory. The notion 'particular" shall be avoided here because it already represents a conceptual placement within a relation. Nonetheless, we must penetrate to the original experiences and their various relationships to our own states. To make this clear, suppose we are observing a lime tree. Everything about this form that is relational has been thought, is conceptual, and thus produced by thinkers. Everything that is not conceptual and thus first brought into relation via concepts appears to the observers as something not produced by them, but rather present without their contribution, as something which they receive. To become aware of the tree's form, the apprehender is productive as well as receptive in various ways. A considerable effort of impartiality is required to make this clear with sufficient exactness. It is all too easy to deceive oneself about the relevance of this distinction by assuming that it is simply obvious and unavoidable that we receive certain elements of our consciousness and produce others. Nonetheless, one of the most far-reaching resolutions of our epistemological endeavors is to proceed from the indeterminateness of the familiar to a clear answer to the question of what is produced and what is received in a given instance, and then to consistently pursue this distinction to the limit of decidability. Upon closer inspection one notices that not only spatial relationships of the tree's form (above, below, right, left, front, back) bring the tree's parts and partial wholes (which are in turn conceptually determined) into a conceptual relation. Rather, this also applies to the qualitative or modal determinations. The green we attribute to the leaf is a concept of the same type as that of "tree," "branch," or "above." All these concepts share the same universality with respect to the objects as well as to the human acts of thinking which apprehend them. When we direct our gaze to a green leaf, what we apprehend as its real green is neither the universal conceptual green, nor is it the perceptual differentiation of its surface in its segregated multiplicity, which we integrate into a whole. The real green is the unification of *both* these elements into a *determinate* green, which, in its uniqueness, is both holistic and manifold. Like all other concepts, the concept green determines its relation to other concepts (such as color, light, dark, contrast, and saturation) through its own content. It also has this double universality in common with other concepts. The non-conceptual component of the *real* green holds the conceptual green in a unification of the conceptual universal with the perceptual non-universal.[5] In this way the representation of a particular green emerges out of the universal green. After the process of unification, this representation can be remembered independently of the perceptual elements in relation to which it was formed. It is the concept with its determinate reference to the perceptual. This reference is acquired through becoming aware of the perceptual components of the green leaf. This happens in the immediate awareness, however, and not only afterward in the remembered representation. Thus, the realm of representation does not only stand for something else (as in the case of memories and intentions). Rather, it extends into objectivity and is necessary for its construction. The implications that this has for a structure-phenomenological treatment of representation shall be addressed below. The perceptual elements of a form are conveyed via the diverse modalities of our neurosensory system. As such, they are modally diverse. However, this modal diversity is not a primary criterion of objectivity. Rather, it likewise acquires form only when the percepts are unified with the concepts of their modality which integrate them into the network of their coherence. The construction of form always consists of a mutual interplay of productive apprehension of conceptual formative elements and receptive taking up of formless perceptual elements. Formation proceeds gradually in this manner. All coherence is of a conceptual, not a perceptual nature.

---

[5] Only gaze-directing forms of expressing that are negative with respect to content can be used to characterize the non-conceptual element.

If we wish to acquire an undistorted understanding of the nature of the basic structure it is necessary to satisfy ourselves by impartial observation that its elements, that is, percepts and concepts, occur as primary given entities, and that they alone elucidate each other. All other attempts at derivation result in absurdities inasmuch as they invariably presuppose these two elements and by including them annul the attempt at explanation. Suspending the function of our sense organs shows that percepts certainly occur only in connection with this function. However, cause and effect must not be mistaken for each other. The function of our sense organs is a condition for the occurrence of percepts, and not their cause (and for its own part causally affected), as the affection theory would have it. As is the case with all other perceptions, what is perceptible about the sense organs requires percepts and conceptual completion. The formation of a Gestalt is invariably the primary process and cannot be explained by something secondary but rather constitutes the basis of every explanation. In all phenomena, everything coherence-forming and universal is a concept, while everything incoherent and non-universal is a percept. The universal conceptual becomes individualized by the non-universal perceptual, whereas the non-universal perceptual becomes universalized by the universal conceptual, that is, it is integrated into an unboundedly expanding conceptual fabric.

This allows us to see the constitution of the basic structure not as a reality determined prior to human knowing, but rather as a reality gradually formed in becoming aware. Therefore, our generation of form is the continually performed act that creates reality. Although this act is usually performed subconsciously, it can be made conscious through introspective observation. However, this "making conscious" cannot have "Gestalt perception" as its object, because a theoretical approach which assumes that forms are perceptually given entities presupposes that particulars and coherences are objectively homogenous; it therefore cannot be regarded as scientific. Rather, becoming aware of the basic structure concerns construction in a transitive, active sense.

1.3 Explanatory Remarks

Before this short characterization of the basic structure is elaborated further, two explanatory remarks are in order. They are appropriate here because contemporary habits of thought are largely materialistic.

a *Abstraction Theory*. Although the conjecture that the conceptual elements of the generation of form are abstracted, that is, derived by collating uniformities from the non-conceptual elements,[6] is contested, it still exerts a persuasive influence on prevailing opinion. According to the theory's own presuppositions, conceptual abstractions would be possible if perceivable uniformities existed. Especially in regard to this conjecture, it is worth emphasizing the merit of presuppositionless observation. Yet instead of identities, this observation shows differences, insofar as the perceptual is under consideration. Moreover, observation in the direction of the perceptible ends where we can no longer differentiate. Two supposedly identical objects (e.g., two circles) are

---

[6][Piaget & Inhelder, 1969]

not perceptually identical—were it so, there would only be a *single* circle. In the two instances, only the differently individualized concept is identical. We can convince ourselves of this by observing countless other instances of this sort. If uniformity is asserted, then this is a conceptual addition to the perceptible, and not borrowed from it. The abstraction theory attempts to derive the concept from the percept via something it adds to it.

b *Physiological Theory.* With respect to refuting the conjecture that concepts emerge via physiological functions, the crucial insight is gained from the explanatory function of concepts. This function is only successful because concepts stand in relation to one another due to their own content and its specific correspondences, that is, because the concepts themselves do not need explaining. Only when self-explanatory elements are present is explanation possible at all.[7] Only that which is self-explanatory can establish the coherence of the non-self-explanatory perceptible. Since coherences can only be explained by their own formation of coherence, all attempts to explain their occurrence based on other elements must fail because such attempts make use of the explanatory function of thinking. If one claims to explain conceptual coherence via extra-conceptual coherence, then one is using conceptual elements in the explanation. This

---

[7]It is not necessary here to go into Tarski's paradox of self-explanation [Tarski, 1983] nor the paradoxes of set theory [e.g., Russell, 1967], which are easily solved by structure phenomenology.

explanation, however, presupposes that which it purports to explain, whilst at the same time denying that which it explains. The conjecture that there must be an extra-conceptual cause for conceptual coherence may well seem plausible to contemporary habits of thought. Nevertheless, it cannot appeal to the fact that human thinking acts without concurrent physiological processes has not been established (e.g., neuroelectrical correlates under the influence of what is called the P300 component[8]); for although the apprehension of thought content through thinking acts is contingent on physiological functions, it is not caused by them. This follows from the contrast between the structuring function of the conceptual capacity and the destructuring processes of the human neurosensory system, which only convey incoherent percepts. Moreover, thinking acts are distinct from self-explanatory thought contents, which, by explaining themselves, stand in a relation of reciprocal determination to the thinking acts. They represent an autonomous realm, impervious to heteronomous determination. A presuppositionless view of the basic structure gained by introspective observation can persuade anyone of the absurdity of a conjecture that uses something self-explanatory to derive the self-explanatory from something non-self-explanatory. Moreover, because this conjecture proceeds from the materialistic assumption of the objective homogeneity of particulars and coherences, it unwittingly denies the very

---

[8][Chapman & Bragdon, 1964]

possibility of explanation. On the one hand, with respect to the relation of these two elements to the contents of consciousness, it can only give the absurd answers already considered, whilst, on the other hand, the question regarding the relationship between particular and relation remains unanswered.

2

The Crucial Difficulty. The Problem of Generation

The area of research of structure phenomenology has been outlined by characterizing the basic structure and rejecting assumptions that deny it or fail to even consider it. The task of structure phenomenology, then, is to show via concepts individualized through observations the variations in which the basic structure appears, both in individual cases and classes of cases. This results in research questions that relate to the nature of specific structures as well as questions that address the procedure of structure phenomenology and its epistemic feasibility. It follows, namely from the basic structure that the method to be employed can be neither inductive nor deductive but rather must be productive-indicative (in the sense of the epistemic productive participation in what is known). It is now time to address the resultant difficulties.

a. *Self-giving. Temporalization. Depresentification.*[1] Anyone familiar with the generative character of the basic structure is aware of a problem that likewise arises with respect to thinking, that is the formation of concepts. What is produced (be it the basic structure or thinking itself) can only be observed as such after it has been produced. Coupled with this seemingly harmless premise are considerable difficulties which can initiate profound and far-reaching investigation.

1 The correct assessment of the difficulty just mentioned is the condition of understanding the following discussion as well as the intention of this treatise; the intention is namely to clarify the relationship between naïve consciousness and the reliable consciousness of reality unencumbered by decisions made in advance. A path shall be shown which reaches its destination between naïve realism and affectionist illusionism and also accurately matches the subjective and objective parts of the content of our consciousness to each other. This is considered to be the *main epistemological task* here.

2 If we wish to obtain a fundamental scientific clarification of this kind, we can best begin by ascertaining that the aforementioned difficulty cannot arise in the same manner for a solely receptive mode of becoming aware. Rather, it is characteristic of *generative cognition*. For observation whose objects were fully predetermined by processes of whatever

---

[1] [Witzenmann's use of precisely these three terms is certainly due to his preoccupation with Heidegger (1962), but here they appear in a methodical and conceptual context that is quite different from Heidegger.]

kind (i.e., processes distinct and independent of those active in becoming aware) the arising of its objects would have a very different significance compared to observation whose objects arise through our own generation. An observing activity whose objects occur via the formative processes of the basic structure is of a similar kind to that active in the construction of objects. The terms "heteronomous" and "autonomous" can be used to distinguish these two types of observation without first deciding whether they are possible. Then it is the case that for heteronomous observation the causes of the arising of its objects would lie outside its scope of generative action. Equivalently, because the activity of autonomous observation takes part in the arising of both partners, it encompasses the autonomous observation itself and its objects. The relation between the arising of objects and their observation is then characterized by the fact that they belong to the same area of activity. It should be explained on the basis of the characterization of the generative form of the basic structure that we do not receive prefabricated structures, but rather productively take part in their arising. The hypothetical assumption of two types of objects with corresponding types of observation was only intended to elucidate the dependency of objectivity on the basic structure. The conjecture that there is observation or knowledge that is heteronomous not only in fact in specific instances, but rather necessarily in accordance with the constitution of possible objects must be rejected on two grounds; namely, on the one hand, because this conjecture leads to the contradictions of the affection, resemblance, homogeneity, abstraction, and physiological theories, and, on the other hand, because presuppositionless observation demonstrates the generative form of the basic structure.

3 In the aforementioned unification of the perceptual and conceptual, process and result must be distinguished. The process brings the separate components together, and the result is their accomplished fusion. We call this result an *object*. However, this does not yet characterize the concept of object; it shall be clarified later. So far, it has only been said under what conditions objects occur. Objects in this sense are not only what we refer to as articles of daily use such as tables and chairs, but also their parts, and in the broad sense also everything that comes under our observation as something formed, such as houses, cliffs, mountains, living beings, and their parts. Further, everything that has acquired form through the unification of the perceptual and conceptual is objective, for example surfaces and temperatures, but also sensations and emotions insofar as their perceptual element is conceptually determined. The purely perceptual and purely conceptual are also observable. But how and by what means such observation is possible must be established in the following discussion. Establishing the fact that observation occurs does not yet yield its concept. Rather, this concept must also emerge in the course of the exposition. The aforementioned distinction between process and result defines an important question for our investigation, namely the question of the relationship between objects (the unified form of percept and concept as result) and their presupposition (the unification of percept and concept as process). This question concerns both the type of relation between these formative levels as well as its possibility. The conditions and difficulties of an answer now need to be clarified.

4   The question of the relationship between process and result is ancient. It has been part of a diligent and veracious endeavor since this endeavor freed itself from lethargic and timid acquiescence and took up the questions of *being* and *becoming*. The problems of *duration* on the one hand, and *coming to be* and *passing away* on the other are of general scientific interest. It would greatly exceed the scope of this treatise to explore them in their many ramifications.[2] Rather, within the confines of the inquiry undertaken here, the question of generation and emergence shall be pursued in the interconnection of the formation of structure, observation, and objectivity. It will become apparent that this particular observation will shed light on a much larger area.

5   A further stage of the deliberation can be dedicated to the following peculiarity of the basic structure. Because of its universal validity, what arises through the unification of its elements, namely percept and concept, is not something completely new, but rather something that, *with respect to the*

---

[2] The author has outlined this area of inquiry in the article "Erkenntniswissenschaftliche Bemerkungen zum Bewegungsproblem" [Epistemological remarks on the problem of motion] [Witzenmann, 1977].

basic structure, is *always the same*. What we unquestioningly take to be the familiar objective present is always the result and occurrence of the same structural processes. With continuous processes and movement (see footnote 2) the each result is preceded by a movement phase that is just past. (A remark on the problem of continuity will be made below.) The structural result is a process of construction in which each of the two elements simultaneously forms and is formed by the other. Thus, their difference must remain, albeit in an altered form, and nothing completely different from them can arise, as in the case of chemical compounds. What is new in the equation $H_2 + O = H_2O$ is not structurally new because the basic structure of each of the five parts of the equation remains the same in its characteristic application.[3] Accordingly, formation, which is the unification of its structural elements (percept and concept), can only exhibit the characteristic of these two formative elements. When these elements modify each other, the type of modification is nevertheless characteristic of each modifying element. Processes of chemical binding do not result in a new but rather a modified basic structure. What is new here are the perceptual and conceptual ingredients that (as always) enter into the connecting structure, which is not chemical but phenomenal. Once this is recognized, we learn about the inexhaustibility of the structural resources as well as the

---

[3]The justification or interpretation of the equals sign cannot be discussed here.

permanence of the basic structure.[4] Modifications do not contradict the basic structure, but are rather structurally conditioned by it.

6   However, the objects we observe do not seem to have the constitution that is expected if they are to be regarded as occurrences of the basic structure. What our objectifying supposition ascertains, or believes it ascertains contains no indication of our generative participation. Rather, all objects seem to approach us as something finished so that we can make no contribution to their formation. Objectness seems to possess the characteristics of a more or less permanent state and of integration in the environment reciprocally conditioned by itself and the environment. It seems to stand as something self-determined in relation to a similarly determined environment. This also seems to be the case for moving objects (a thrown ball, a flying bird, running water) as movement presupposes the objective determinacy of that

---

[4] The double motif of being and becoming, which permeates this treatise more or less below the surface, also becomes clear in this regard. The lawfulness of formation, which is constant in its mode of being, is replenished by inexhaustible sources of elements that are continually entering in realization anew from two sides. In this way structural being, which remains constant in change, arises out of becoming. Thus, development, which is a unification of becoming and being, is something different from these levels that constitute its formation. The process of formation in question here is not *only* subjective. It is the participatory act of the process of realization. For it has become manifest that the attempts to circumvent the formation of structure fail because it cannot be fathomed and is itself their ground. The formation of structure is therefore the participatory act of the process that forms reality. The formation of structure has the moving function yet remains itself unchanged because it is the processual form of the uniform occurrence of reality. However, that which is unmoved in its mode of occurring can nevertheless be moved by that which it moves, should the latter lend it a new form of expression. The transformative range of evolution contains this possibility. For human beings provide their own reality through the participation in the process of realization. Thus, they usher in a new epoch of consequential events.

which is moving. The characteristics of determinacy of state and of integration in an environment are equivalent to the supposed *presence* of objects. We speak of "presence" where we consider these characteristic requirements fulfilled. The presence of objects seems to be self-sufficient. It does not seem to contain any indication that its coming into being is dependent on us, nor does it seem to need this.

7 If the formation of the basic structure really does take place with our active participation, then to suppose that the presence of objects is independent of our own activity must be a *mistaken interpretation*. Structural formation and independent objectness are not reconcilable with each other. If one is the case, then the other is not. This interpretation of objectivity, however, though rendered understandable by its generative form, is not justified by it. This is because all events (i.e., successive occurrences that constitute a whole process) are subject to the *law of temporalization*. This entails that an occurrence within a series and its previous and successive occurrences exclude each other. The occurrence of objectness excludes its prior process of generation. Hence, if our observation is restricted to becoming aware of objectness, then we lack the knowledge with which we could judge its generative form. The missing connection cannot be found by bringing in other objects since with them the same deficit would arise and an infinite regress would result.

8 This means that the observation of the effect of structuring cannot simultaneously apprehend the process of structuring and also that we would never be able to observe the formation

of structure if our observation were restricted to its results. The same problem arises in connection with moving objects and beings (a thrown ball, a flying bird). A single occurrence within a movement series excludes the movement itself, which consequently cannot be apprehended by apprehending the individual occurrences (cf. footnote 2).[5] In order to apprehend the relation of objectness to its structural generation we would hence need a type of observation that, *free from the law of temporalization*, can complement the object-related mode of observation. It would make the correct interpretation of the object-related mode of interpretation possible for the first time because what is objective is already temporalized and has fallen out of the *context* of temporalization. That we really possess such a faculty of observation is demonstrated by our awareness of movement even if we have not taken its use into account and it therefore remains subconscious (cf. footnote 2). As we do not make common use of it in structural processes, we must ask whether we can make use of it here at all. A judgment regarding objectness is, however, clearly only possible when we have observations and judgments based on such observations at our disposal that are not subject to the law of temporalization. The possibility of such observation and judgment must therefore be demonstrable if an appraisal of objectness in terms of the basic structure and statements related to it are permissible.

---

[5][Bergson, 1912]

9   This problem can be further clarified by means of the concept of *self-giving*. The formation of the basic structure as participation in the formation of objects (reality) is equivalent to self-giving. We ourselves give to our observation that which we bring about. What is thus brought about stands therefore in relation to that which we ourselves earlier participated in. Our relations to our own earlier participation are memories. Consequently, objectivity must, with regard to this participation, be judged as memory and its presence separate from us exposed to be a mistaken interpretation in favor of its *memorative form*.

10 This rectification is only possible if *two conditions* are fulfilled: Firstly, objectivity must really have a memorative form; our habitual supposition of objects balks vehemently at this; and, secondly, its memorative form must not only be real, but also be apprehensible, and its apprehensibility demonstrable. This seems questionable as it entails that observation is possible which is independent of temporalization and does not objectify because at the moment of objectification the *process* of objectification is not yet or no longer existent. For the required rectification is to be viable, two *further conditions* must be fulfilled: Firstly, a mode of observation and judgment must be possible that invalidates the supposition of presence and apprehends the memorative form of objectivity, that is one that depresentifies. Secondly, in addition to this, a mode of observation and judgment must also be possible which apprehends the *conditions* of objectness, that is, again one that depresentifies, because it goes behind objectness. This

characterizes the *law of depresentification*, which applies to observation and results from a generative cognition. Only if the validity of this law is established can the memorative form of objectivity be verified.

11 The preceding discussion can be *summarized* as follows: The basic structure and the supposition of presence *contradict* each other. This contradiction is maintained not only by the stubbornness of habit, but also because its resolution seems at least to be hindered by the problems associated with structure generation, if it is not indeed rendered impossible. It can only be resolved if the memorative form of the objective that results from *self-giving* can be verified. In this context it is necessary to explain why the *relation to something not present*, which is determinative of remembering and has to be expected if objects have a memorative form, usually does not or does not seem to arise in becoming aware of objects. This brings up the *paradox* that self-giving demands a memorative form of its result whilst at the same time excluding the possibility of its apprehension via an act directed at its result. Verification of the memorative form of objects can only succeed if the validity of the *law of depresentification* is verifiable. This would, on the one hand, verify the *law of temporalization* with regard to the memorative form of objects and, on the other, be expressed in a mode of observation and judgment of the conditions of objectivity that is not subject to the law of temporalization. In connection with depresentification it is necessary to make the supposition of presence understandable as a *mistaken interpretation*.

As both the basic structure and its conceptual elements arise through acts, this investigation must now consider memory and its structure. This will make it clear that memory phenomena play a central role for structure phenomenology.

b. *A Seemingly Resultant Infinite Regress.* A further difficulty concerns the memorative form itself, because memories are entities formed out of coherencies and incoherencies and therefore have the same, though faded, structure as the supposedly present objects. With respect to the generative construction of memories it seems impossible to avoid the prospect that memories must also be remembered. This would result in a regress that is extremely pernicious with respect to apprehension, excluding forever the possibility of coming to a full awareness of objects.

c. *The Problem of Continuity.* There is not even any reassurance in taking refuge in banality, for it can indeed be claimed that the persistence of the results of generation after the generative process is just as well known to us as the process itself and the associated memory. Similarly, in producing letters with a writing instrument, both the process and the result would be observed, and the process remembered. This objection attempts to explain the explanandum by recourse to its presupposition, for it presupposes forms and movements without considering their structural constitution. The research problem relating to structure, however, is precisely the interpretation of objectivity and movement. Moreover, in relation to the question of the memorative form of objectivity it is concerned not with a concomitant, but rather a structural remembering. The structure of movement and form are modes of appearance of the *structure of continuity* (of the transition of functions leading to holistic structures which continually arise from differentiated elements). This analysis is of major scientific interest. The problem of transition will be considered in the following discussion to the extent the confines of this treatise allow. It is clear from the discussion thus far that the problems encountered are insoluble as long as the problem of generation that permeates them remains unsolved. Although the theoretical decomposition of a process into many static moments can be of help in practical applications, it does not contribute to the problem of continuity, rather in this respect it is a deception. If one claims one is directly certain of objectivity (and similarly motion) and its emergence, then this only proves that one is not able to recognize the problem outlined here. It is precisely this supposition of certainty that seems to be incompatible with structural observation. The interpretation of objectivity (the holistic continuity) is twice confronted with the problem of generation, on the one hand via the generation of the conceptual elements of structure, and on the other hand via the generation of structures themselves.

3
The Proposed Solution

3.1 Thinking Act and Thought Content (Evidence)

If it is at all possible to overcome the difficulties outlined above, then it is only possible with the help of concepts. Thus, recourse to concepts is necessary. However, as the consideration of thinking and its objects seem to be entangled in the problem of generation and remembering, the difficulties present themselves anew.

Nevertheless, the distinction between *thinking act* and *thought content* can help us along. The peculiar difference and interrelation between them is of a significance that is usually not correctly assessed.

Thinking acts are acts of particular people at particular times. As such they are, with respect to their origin, subjective and raise the previously mentioned questions that for their part relate to the questions of generation and temporalization. Hence, this deliberation has again reached the point at which the question of the compatibility of generation, memorative form, and objectivity must be addressed.

This does not apply, however, to *thought contents*, which form a self-contained coherence; for they are coherent through themselves and need not and cannot be made to cohere by other means. A concept is not just an element of a particular coherence as, for example, "up" and "down" are spatial relations. Rather, each concept is also part of a universal ideational coherence because persisting and flowing in coherence is an essential characteristic of concepts and, therefore, conceptual coherence is nowhere interrupted. The concepts receive their determinations from their participation in the universal ideational coherence. These determinations, though transferable to percepts, are nevertheless governed by a super-conceptual totality. These are therefore forms of appearance of a universal coherence, to which transitory thinking acts that happened at a particular time are irrelevant. Rather, the temporal determinations "now," "earlier," and "later" are elements of the universal coherence, which is itself not temporal but rather superordinate to temporal determinations. Likewise, the temporal determinations themselves are superordinate to their temporal individualization in relation to percepts in a super-temporal universality and a super-temporal participation in the totality. Through their thinking acts human beings connect with the thought contents as elements of the universal coherence and thus determine its appearance in a specific conceptual form. At the same time, however, in performing a thinking act the thinker is also determined by the apprehended conceptual element, whose placement in the conceptual coherence cannot be changed and which rather carries itself over into the thinker's own thinking activity. These reciprocal determinations of the selecting human thinking activity and the self-ordering conceptual content form the significance of evidence (whose demonstrability is often contested). This provides an insightfulness that includes human accessibility among its intrinsic determinations (i.e., not augmentable through others) via their reciprocal determination. Hence, evidence contains no elements that are not simultaneously determining and reciprocally determined. This identity of determination and reciprocal determinateness is perfectly intelligible and transparent. From this starting point the problem of generation is solvable.

3.2 Further Elucidation on This Approach to a Solution

To render this understandable further elucidation is necessary.

  a *The Impossibility of Remembering Evidence.* The evidential content of pure concepts cannot be remembered because prior to individualization the content of pre-individualized concepts is independent of, indeed separate from, their temporal actualization. However, memory is only possible in temporal relation to objectified phenomena. Where the content of consciousness excludes this relation remembering does not occur. As universal concepts cannot be remembered they must, insofar as they appear, always be apprehended anew, and indeed always are. What can be remembered are the attendant circumstances when concepts are apprehended; among them are also the acts themselves. Each of these rememberable acts is certainly temporalized in its initiation. However, it passes over into an awareness of an unrememberable super-temporality that is not subject to the law of temporalization. The reason an act can be considered rememberable is precisely because there are apprehensible determinations which do not pass away as the act itself does, but remain valid independent of time. Through such super-temporal determinations the act obtains its temporal determination, namely of actualizing a concept whose content is prior to its actualization.

b *Two Types of Observation.* Where thinking activity passes over into evidence further observations can be made which are necessary for understanding the formation of structure. A distinction follows from what has been said that must be taken into account when considering the manner in which the structuring activity takes part in the building of structure. In the formation of evidence, that which can currently be remembered passes over into that which is universally unrememberable. This results in the possibility of judgments that are independent of temporal conditions and solely determined by their conceptual content. In contrast, the non-conceptual, perceptible element presents that which is inaccessible and impenetrable to our structuring activity. Our activity is unable to provide evidence with respect to this element. This attentive activity that leads to awareness is called observation. In the case of pure, non-individualized concepts observation passes over into evidence. In the case of the non-conceptual, perceptible element observation does not pass over, and instead stops in front of that which is non-evident. This provides a new criterion for distinguishing conceptual and non-conceptual elements in the construction of structure. The type of observation, that is the observation of observation, sheds light on this: the two elements can be distinguished based on the difference in the observation directed to them. This investigation will return to this later. This also demonstrates the previously postulated distinction between two types of observation that are directed toward the objective and non-objective, respectively (process and result), whereby the observation directed at the non-objective itself appears in two forms.

c *Metamorphoses of Concepts as Features of Structure.* Likewise, observation of the way in which concepts integrate into structures leads to important distinctions. Concepts cannot only be *actualized* to yield evidence, but can also be *intentionalized*, that is, they can be employed for the purpose of formation of structure in observation directed toward the non-evident. Then, through actualization and intentionalization, they are already pre-individualized for the formation of structure. Whether they can enter into or inhere in a structurally closed individualization depends on whether their individualization arises through a perceptible, observable imprint (not through conjecture) and can connect itself without contradiction to the individualization of other concepts that arose in the same manner. Hence, the mark of success is the structure's progressing degree of individualization (its degree of inherence). The pre-individualized concepts are perspectives on the purely perceptible, attitudes toward it, purposeful patterns of behavior. Where they are missing (e.g., in the moment of shock) nothing is perceived. Actualized and intentionalized concepts are features of structure.

d *The Problem of Transition.* A related consideration concerns the *transition* from the non-individualized or merely pre-individualized concepts into their individualized, structuring form. The question of transition is of general epistemological interest, which cannot be satisfied in its full extent here.[1] However, it is immediately clear that this transition can only occur when the universal concepts can be adapted to the individual perceptual conditions. That they are capable of adaptation in this way follows from the fact that representations are indeed formed: we do not only have the universal (evidential) concept "fir tree" at our disposal, but also (individualized and adapted) representations of specific fir trees, which can represent fir trees without necessarily observing their perceptual constituents. Further, in our "inner" representational activity, we can form series of representations of conceptually related forms that are adapted forms of the same universal concept. Hence, concepts can be *metamorphosed.*

---

[1] Goethe, with his usual genius and penetrating mind, pointed to the problem of transition as the fundamental epistemological problem. "Here we meet the real difficulty, one we do not always see clearly: between idea and experience there inevitably yawns a chasm which we struggle to cross with all our might, but in vain. In spite of this we are forever in search of a way to overcome this gap with reason, intellect, imagination, faith, feeling, delusion, and—when all else fails—folly" [Goethe, 1988, p. 33]. Structure Phenomenology decides on the criterion of truth, whose significance for all knowing Goethe addresses with the pathos of someone who knows, but is unable to bring to full consciousness the insight that is decisive for the fate of knowledge.

e *Individualization.* The inherence phase of concepts follows the adaptation phase. In the inherence phase the main concept of a structure, together with other concepts subject to it, inheres in the perceptual field and is held in it such that structure is formed. The quality of inherence of a structure increases with the conceptual subordination systematics. The structured form only arises through inhering. However, structures can only arise because the conceptual elements can appear in various forms that continuously merge into one another and conditionally relate to each other. Concepts can *inhere*.

f *Rejecting a Prejudice.* Before proceeding further in this investigation a prejudice shall be considered which is deeply imbedded in prevailing habits of thought. The view being advocated here, which is based on the self-explanatory autonomy of concepts, could be challenged with the claim that children acquire their concepts from their experiences that they have with objects. (A burnt child dreads the fire.) If this objection is being made in the sense of the abstraction theory (in which concepts are taken to be merely subjective representatives of non-conceptual givens), then it has already been considered. This objection connects the abstraction theory with the homogeneity theory via the common pre-existence of particulars and coherences for cognition, which has already been refuted. It is nevertheless the case that the child selects concepts out of the ideational realm, that is acquires concepts on the basis of experiences it has with forms of our world. However, this does not occur by learning to derive concepts from pre-existing structures as the refuted conceptions suppose. Rather the child only has experiences to the extent it has acquired (though not necessarily consciously accounted for) the ability to apply concepts to percepts and thus to form structure. It reaches for the moon as long as it is unable to structure its surroundings via the concepts which construct spatial objects. Through the application of concepts the child becomes acquainted with the nature of concepts as well as with the character of its surroundings. It has experiences of concepts and objects not by deriving concepts from predetermined structures, but by trying out the structuring function of concepts in the construction of structures, that is in the formation of an idealized world out of the idealess perceptible. What is won on the basis of specific experiences is, with regard to evidence, not dependent on what is experienced. Rather, what is experienced is dependent on evidence.

3.3 Formation of Reality and Beings

The foregoing remarks provide an overview of the structuring function of the different conceptual forms and their relation to each other.

Concepts are characterized by their possibility to be

i *Actualized* (apprehended through a reciprocal determining activity), whereby evidence arises (the production of something determined by its own lawfulness),

ii *Intentionalized* (behavior-specific directedness that in itself points beyond itself to what is thus and only to this extent perceptible (non-evident)); structuring activity (reciprocal determining activity) thus gains the specific observationally directed relation to the elements that to this extent are non-conceptual (non-evidential), which only then become observable,

iii *Metamorphosed* (adapted in a continuously variable manner to a class of figures with a similar form or a sequence of forms that comprise a figure); the concepts are thus susceptible to adaptation to, and suitable for the transition to specific percepts and perceptual fields, and

iv *Inherent* (separately (individually) adaptable to specific perceptual fields, which the concepts form and by which they themselves are formed, that is a forming formability); the structures, formed out of conceptual and non-conceptual elements, thus arise.

The conceptual metamorphosis is a stepwise transition of the evidential to the non-evidential. Each stage is determined by the preceding stage and the direction of transition. Within this context of conditionality the specific nature of each stage becomes understandable. Because the stages explain each other, their sequence, which comprises the transition, is understandable through itself. However, this presentation is restricted to ascertaining that the transition does indeed occur. How and why the possibility of a transition from the universal to the non-universal has its ground in the universal itself must be addressed in a presentation specifically dedicated to the problem of universals.[2] However, it may be apparent from what has been expounded thus far that this account of

---

[2][Although Witzenmann has not published an extensive work on this subject, references can be found in Witzenmann, 1986, 1989a, 1994.]

the metamorphosis of concepts (the universal of universals) represents the completion of Goethe's doctrine of metamorphosis.

It is clear that the sequence of requirements that bring about structure is the same for all formation of structure. The transition of the elements generating coherence to a structure can only proceed from evidence in the direction of inherence. Hence, all phenomena are embedded within the same universal context of formation because only through the modification of evidential elements into inherences can structures arise. The fact that our active participation in the arising of structure does not render it a merely subjective process follows from the fact that we connect ourselves reciprocally-determinately in evidence with self-determining elements.

When considering the formation of structures it is necessary to distinguish between process and result with respect not only to the formal structure but also to the perceptible contents. Although all phenomena result from the same universal process of formation, this process finds different expression in different beings and different classes of beings. In the realm of inorganic forms only the inherent form of structuring elements comes into effect. This is the reason for the rigidity of these forms; the scope of their structure does not include the variability of the universal concept but instead only fixates its individualized form. These forms can therefore only be changed via external influences. (Crystals are transitional forms.) With organisms the change of form is a part of the construction of their form. In this case, the form is a sequence of forms that is unified in a larger formal coherence to a whole. However, it is certainly insufficient to speak of a "temporal form" in respect to organisms because the forms of inorganic nature also undergo change through time without losing their characteristic form (at least within certain limits). Rather, an appropriate judgment of organisms must take up the organological criterion according to which the individual being is able to metamorphose the concept in such a way that its formation itself is subject to the higher principle of the change of form such that the change of form is itself its formation. Animals are characterized by the fact that their behavior expresses the possibility that a concept can be intentionalized. Nevertheless, unlike human beings their intentional patterns of behavior are not determinable by the cognitive capacities of the individual, but rather are expressions of rigid species-specific drivenness. It is only in the human being that all elements of the construction of structure, including the stage in which concepts can be actualized as evidence, are constitutively united. Therefore, human beings continuously participate subconsciously in all phases of the construction of the form of beings that they encounter in their sphere of observation. In the exceptional state of fully aware observation they are able to become conscious of the complete formation of the forms that populate their environment and of the structural peculiarity of this formation. They thus gain the insight that, through the conscious participation in the structures, they are working on the construction of their own essence and, in a specific sense, predetermine its further development. Let me explain this further.

Only a few indications have been given here regarding the particular nature of the forms of our world. The various types of form and their typical realms include areas that present a multitude of unsolved problems for structure-phenomenological research (with respect to both the acquisition of evidential content as well as its individuation); extensive endeavor will be necessary to explore this.

The main concern here has been to establish that there is a logical sequence of structuring elements which is run through in each instance of formation of structure and indeed must occur due to the constitution of the basic structure. Individual beings and their realms are positioned differently within this general dynamic of form inasmuch as not all of their functional elements belong to the inner dimension of their particular typical structure. Rather, individual elements of the basic structure can, in specific cases, also belong to the outer dimension of the structure of beings. Hence, it is necessary to distinguish the following classes of formation of structure:

1. The *basic structure* as the unification of perceptual and conceptual elements;
2. The *evidence* as unification of thinking acts with thought contents;
3. The *transition* of the structuring concepts in the sequence from actualized to inherent form;
4. The *structure of the typical forms* (or beings) and the *realms of forms*, whose own structure does not always include all the conceptual transitional forms, but because of the universal requirements of formation of structure for the transition is located within the structure of reality. This results in inner and outer morphogenetic functions.

Because the unification of percept and concept is called cognition, the participation in the entire structuring sequence of transitional forms is the *structure of knowledge*. This structure is given by the generative participation in the universal structuring conditions of origin in which all beings are embedded. The morphogenesis involved in cognition can be called the *structure of the world, or of reality*, for all of the above conditions apply to all beings, even though not all take part in the inner formation of each being. It is therefore necessary to distinguish between the structure of a being and its placement within the structure of the world. Human beings stand in a distinguished relationship to the structure of the world, for all constitutive elements of the structure of the world are united, albeit in an individualized form, in their constitution. Further, the nature of their special status includes the fact that when they take a cognition-like or cognitive attitude, they unconsciously participate in the world structure and the particular nature of its activity in every individual being. But they can also observe consciously and cognitively co-create the world structure. In cognizant co-creation they construct their own spiritual being and acquire the ability to develop it further through free acts of self-formation; for they determine the content of their spiritual being themselves through the manner and extent to which they acquire evidence. They change and strengthen their power of self-formation to the extent to which they become conscious of their epistemic ability.

The preceding is an outline of the metamorphosis of the phenomena (though only in broad strokes). Goethe strove for a presentation of this universal metamorphosis, but could only complete it in certain fields. It is evident from the outline given here that it is the same *archetypal form* whose metamorphoses appear as the structure of the world, the structure of the beings or objects, and the structure of human cognition. Further, this outline shows that the human being, based on participation in the basic structure, grants this archetype a new mode of efficacy in his or her own being.

3.4 The Sub-temporal and Super-temporal

The overview of the structure-phenomenological sequence of formation and conditioning results in conceptions of reality, of the human being and of knowledge. This results further in the structure-phenomenological concepts of formation of a being, of behavior, of adaptation and of judging as a co-performed and observed formation of inherence. For, as unifications of percepts and concepts, the forms of our world, which are formed from inherences, are judgments.

The preceding considerations have alleviated doubts regarding the generative character of structures and the conceptual elements that form structure. For they have led to the insight that structures incorporate elements that are independent of time and are therefore removed from the problem of memory so that we can participate in these elements unaffected by the law of temporality. These super-temporal principles of form permeate the process of formation of structure and thus allow temporally independent judgments that, with respect to their truth, are entirely determined through their self-explanatory content.

Nevertheless, a key question still remains unanswered: While judgments relating to structures certainly pertain to their features, they do not state anything as to how or why awareness of objects in accordance with the arising of structure is possible at all. Judgments about the construction of objectivity state as such nothing about how it comes to awareness. Therefore, the question of memory and its interweaving with the construction of structure arises anew. The structural character of the resulting forms generated by us can only be apprehended in the reminiscent relation to their origin. However, as has already been shown, the following peculiarity arises here from self-giving: While self-giving requires its results to have a memorative form, it simultaneously excludes their apprehension in the same act. If we really mean our awareness of objects, as is continuously the case when we are awake, then valid judgments about this awareness of objects are only possible if we are able to judge on the temporally dependent objective and its relation to the basic structure by virtue of judgments whose contents are independent of time. Thus the problem still remains as to how objectivity is possible with respect to the law of depresentification (leaving aside the paradox of self-giving).

Regarding a solution to the problem of memory it must be pointed out that sub-temporal and super-temporal elements take part in the formation of structure. The pure concepts apprehended in evidence have been characterized as super-temporal, whereas the purely perceptual elements have to be referred to as sub-temporal because they lack all conceptual determination including temporal determination. (Although only a willingness for strenuous observation can render it apparent, it should be emphasized here again that non-conceptuality is the condition for perceptibility and that pure perceptibility is not possible in the absence of concepts; for nothing perceptual can be observed without conceptually directed attention.) Due to the super- and sub-temporality of the complementary elements the temporality of the basic structure only arises through the unification of these elements.[3] The evidential and non-evidential elements can be characterized through super-temporal conceptual coherences (the former directly, the latter

---

[3]This comment on the problem of time must here suffice though it certainly needs a study of its own.

indirectly). Super-temporality is equivalent to the self-determined self-explanation of the conceptual elements, which constitutes an unchanging ideational totality. Through this conceptual self-determination the non-conceptual perceptible element is seen as being universal-conceptually non-determinable. With regard to the evident-conceptual it is therefore not only determined logically as non-conceptual, but also determined factually as unattainable by means of concepts alone; nevertheless it is interpretable only through concepts. The temporal process of structure formation takes place through the unification of the sub-conceptual and super-conceptual. Recollection is interwoven with the awareness of the results of structuring as a result of the generation of this awareness. Thus, it now becomes apparent that a statement about remembering that is itself not caught up in the problematic of memory can be made if it solely demonstrates modifications of super- and sub-temporal elements in the memory structure. It was shown above that with respect to the basic structure the universal elements become individualized, that is modified by the non-universal elements, and, further, that the non-universal elements become universalized, that is integrated into the universal coherence. These are statements that only concern the relation of sub- and super-temporal elements.

3.5 Thinking Act and Self-consciousness (the "I"). The Concept of Observation

The involvement of a temporal act (i.e., thinking activity, which has the role of production) together with self-consciousness connecting with this act still remains problematic. The temporal thinking act determines (actualizes) an element of the universal coherence (i.e., brings it forth) and is reciprocally determined by it. In this way the human act of actualizing becomes itself an element of the ideational coherence. Although the coherence does not contain this element before the completed actualization, this element belongs henceforth to the characteristics of its content. The possibility of actualizing evidential concepts via human acts can be apprehended and addressed as a purely conceptual determination. As has already been shown, the actualized concept can be intentionalized toward the non-conceptual perceptual. The possibility of intentionalizing evident concepts is similarly a determination which belongs to the universal coherence. From this results the concept of an activity that has a twofold expression, corresponding to what was presented above. The concept of an activity that has a twofold expression is itself an element which belongs to the realm of the current evidence and is super-temporally determined. For it concerns the modifications of the universal concepts and thus something that, although it is certainly not originally conceptual, is nevertheless integrated in the ideational coherence. As already mentioned, as such an entity the thinking act is something that is reciprocally determined by its content and in this respect contained in the current evidence. The activity is twofold because it can also turn toward the non-evidential (as directed attention). While this seems to be an original experience, the turn to the non-evidential is directed by means of the same concept that is also encountered as evidential. However, this turn of attention does not only actualize the concept, it also intentionalizes it because nothing can be observed without the orientation- and attention-directing intentionalization of a concept toward something non-conceptual, nothing can be observed without some kind of behavior. The fact that this normally remains subconscious is the vindication of a structure-phenomenological investigation and presentation, whose express task is to render conscious that which is mostly subconscious. In contrast to unification with evidence, the intentionally attention-directed act is the becoming aware of the non-evident from which this attentional act rebounds. As modalities of universals actuality and intentionality are independent of their temporal enactment.

The twofold, unifying and rebounding activity was called "*observation*" above. It can be integrated into the universal or rejected by the non-universal. It is the same structural element which in rebounding undergoes absolute differentiation and in integration via the universal undergoes absolute unification. An ontic entity which appears simultaneously as something differentiated and yet unified, and which attains full consciousness of its unification from its separation when confronted with the non-evidential and determines its separation on the basis of its unification with the evidential, that is stands in an inner relation to itself, calls itself as "I." Thus, I am the one who carries out the unification of concept and percept via the stages of actualizing, intentionalizing, metamorphosing, through to inhering.

The concept of observation has thus been acquired. It is the activity, appearing in various forms, of an "I" apprehending itself. Because it apprehends itself in its own activities, it can, in its self-apprehension, also observe these activities and relate them to each other. This is clearly necessary if the relation between objectivity and the basic structure is to be possible in a way which is itself not objectified (i.e., not memoratively burdened).

3.6 The Solution to the Problem of Memory

The recently developed preliminary deliberations provide the tools for solving the problem of memory:

A. *The Two Dispositions*. A result of the deliberations above is that *two dispositions* arise in the partaking individual through the formation of the basic structure. On the one hand, the inner disposition of the active ability to repeat the individualized conceptuality of the structure is developed. This can be recognized in our ability to remember voluntarily. (The related structural problem of learning and forgetting cannot be addressed here.) On the other hand, a passive disposition also arises in addition to the active disposition. This develops in our organization during the construction of structures (insofar conceptual elements are included in them) by the suppression of the influences of our organization that oppose this process. Because of these influences it is necessary for us (at least subconsciously) to build structures by force of our thinking. These structures then present the phenomena in their reality which had first been decomposed and derealized by our organization. The emergence of the conceptual elements is inhibited when and where our observation rebounds from the non-conceptual elements, which are all that remain of reality after the decomposition brought about by our organization. The trace left by the conceptual repression of our organization's destructuring activity remains imprinted in it with a contour that is blurred, sometimes quickly, sometimes slowly. Thus, contrary to its original destructuring predisposition, our organization acquires dispositions that result from the activity of conceptual elements, that is dispositions to universalize. The searching movements of our resolves to remember, which attempt to find points of connection not contained within themselves, can convince us of the existence of such dispositions. These residues decay with old age or from biological or traumatic impairment according to Ribot's law.[4]

Whereas the active disposition is an individualizing disposition, the passive disposition is a universalizing disposition. Both dispositions develop in the formation of structure. The passive disposition can be called the *disposition of memory* and the active disposition the *disposition of recollection*.

B. *The Memory Structure.* The structure of remembering that consciously appears as such will now be analyzed before investigating whether and how memory-like elements are involved in our seemingly present awareness. This must be postulated due to the generative character of the basic structure. As before, with the memory structure it is necessary to proceed in a manner that is not itself affected by the problem of memory.

Our previously mentioned decisions to remember are possible because the recollective disposition arose due to prior formation of structure. This is the essentially repeatable performative form that our activity had attained in its participation in the transitional stages of evidentially apprehended elements leading up to their inherence. We know of the existence of such recollective dispositions from the successes and failures of our decisions to remember. Using our recollective dispositions, which arise from the influence of the sub-temporal on our capacity to unify with the super-temporal, we search for the dispositions of memory. Our capacity for evidence is developed

---

[4][Ribot, 1882]

further with the formation of structure, and then has an influence on our organic functions, which provide us with our non-evidential percepts. Our dispositions of memory stem from this process. The dispositions of memory represent the other element of the memory structures with which the recollective dispositions must unite during their construction. This element is not, however, of a purely perceptual nature because it has incorporated the universalizing influence complementary to remembering. Correspondingly, the element specific to the recollective disposition is not of a purely conceptual nature because it has been shaped by the individualizing influence. The universalization of the memory dispositions is as such naturally not perceptual; rather, it does not become manifest until a recollective disposition impinges on it. This is in turn affected by the universalization, which stimulates its individualizing nature.

If we resolve to remember, for example, a landscape, then the attempt is from the beginning individualized toward this goal. It does not intend to actualize the general concept of a landscape in order to then subject it to a process of individualization, but rather to imagine an individual landscape with as many universalized particulars as possible that fit into the context of memory. This intention can only guide the decision to remember because the individualizing disposition is pre-existent due to a prior experience. The intentionalized recollective disposition therefore constitutes the starting point of the arising of a memory. However, the intention to remember is successful only to the extent that it is able to unite with the dispositions of memory and take up and organize them in the memory construction. The unification of the recollective dispositions with the memory dispositions in memory representations, which include many particulars, is generally not achieved with complete results on the first attempt, specifically not when it involves memories whose construction makes use of long-term memory. Rather, in most cases the corresponding dispositions of memory are gradually found and incorporated into the developing memory image through a process of reciprocal stimulation of its two constructive functions. This gradual process of completion, which can proceed from many different starting points (e.g., central–peripheral or peripheral–central) and with various focuses of interest, cannot be further explicated here. Also, a memory image that appears richly differentiated when a recollective disposition is exercised for the first time is usually subsequently enriched or modified by various focuses of the recollective attention. Every reasonably careful observation of the emergence of a memory renders the difference between the two essential dispositions clear.

Memory representations are thus structures that arise through a process of construction about which judgments independent of memory can be made through the apprehension of sub- and super-temporal elements. The dispositions can also be characterized in relation to these factors as they are the forms in which the mutual influence of the two elements appears. Memories are therefore not treasures accumulated and ordered in the halls of the mind, as Augustine puts it so vividly in his *Confessions*, treasures that the person remembering can simply summon up, without needing to do anything to construct them; this notion is far removed from the problem at hand. Such a conjecture will never be able to solve the problem of memory.

C. *Memory Structure and Basic Structure.* In observing the memory structure, its particular difference from the basic structure, which merges into objectivity, becomes apparent. In the construction of the basic structure the adaptive universals are individualized in the process of realization by the percepts, which they accept and fit as inherences, whereas the percepts are universalized through the elements that constitute coherence. In the formation of memory structures there is a reversal of this process. With respect to the basic structure one could speak half metaphorically of a contraction of the universals in the perceptual points of consolidation, which function as particulars, and of an expansion of the individualizing influences in the area of the constantly increasing relations. In the case of memories, however, the structuring intentions are already specifically individualized and, in the formation of memory, expand within the obtainable findings of the organization that provides the quasi-perceptual material. Contrary to the original physiological function, the memory-disposed starting points of remembering are universalized to the extent that they already display a quasi-conceptual affinity to the context of memory. Thus, when remembering, the individually predisposed conceptual activity of formation expands, so to speak, into the universally predisposed memory traces, whereas these traces contract, so to speak, into a focus, that is, they are integrated into the specific recollective process. The conceptual and perceptual components of the memory structure (and thus of the form of memory in general) are therefore, in contrast to the basic structure, not only *structurally predisposed*. Moreover, compared to the basic structure the memory structure is *functionally reciprocal* because the previously individualized conceptual component of remembering expands in the previously universalized memory component, which is thereby simultaneously integrated into the individualizing process of remembering, unified by the progressing recollective interest. Thus in the formation of the memory structure a twofold inversion of the corresponding basic structure occurs. The following discussion will comment on the relation of the memory structure to the objective structure to which it corresponds.

3.7 The Deposited Memory Layer. The Concept of Objectivity. The Gaze behind the Veil

Once the memory structure has been characterized in this way (though many related issues must remain unconsidered) it becomes apparent that as the forms of the basic structure enter awareness a memoratively structured layer is, so to speak, *deposited* onto them. In relation to this deposited layer, the basic structure is then a structurally deeper layer and becomes recognizable through this deposited layer as having arisen earlier. A structural finding of this nature was expected from the generative character of the basic structure.

Let me elucidate this introspective observation, which is suited to solve the problem of generation, as follows.

Our contemporary mode of awareness of forms does not pursue the individualization of universals and the universalization of particulars directly. Rather, these processes belong to a deeper and earlier layer of consciousness, which usually remains subconscious. Observers can only penetrate to this layer when, in an exceptional state, they can account for what they initially observed naïvely and superficially. Contrary to the habit that avoids what is essential and intrinsic, we can easily see that unquestioned direct awareness, which is the result of a prior process, does indeed display the expected memorative imprint; for in every instance of supposed direct awareness of objects the partial observations of the object in question are apprehended as an object through the universalizing expansion of a concept, which is already individualized by it, within the contents of the form that belong to it. Moreover, the individual parts of the object are not observed as perceptually isolated entities, but rather as already universalized elements, that is, as parts attributed to the coherence, to the whole, whose members they are. They are apprehended as forms of appearance of one and the same object and as already universalized by the intention that is already individualized. Objective awareness is, on the one hand, an expanding individual apprehension within a manifoldly extended referential verification of the parts. On the other hand, it is the integration of the parts, which are universalized through their referentiality, into the unity given by one and the same intention. The memory layer is deposited in this manner onto the structural basic layer. While the superficial memory layer is, for direct awareness, something earlier, for the exceptional state of introspective observation it is a later product. However, rather than exploring this later product, this exceptional state explores what is subconsciously earlier; this is what imparts self-apprehension and thus depth of experience to memory, which otherwise would remain superficial.

Hence, our normal consciousness is a representational consciousness that is not directly reality-saturated; for this superficial representation is not a representation that is constitutive of the basic structure itself but rather a representation of it via derivative structures. The truth that what is thought to be present is a memory representation cannot remain hidden to our self-observation, which cannot evade its consequences. We can convince ourselves of this with any object. As already mentioned, when we are confronted with an object in a normal stance of consciousness, the previously completed individualization of the pertinent concept (e.g., glass, tree, animal) always directs our observational acts, through which we justify our own awareness to ourselves, toward the object that is already apprehended as such. The result of the observational orientation is therefore the formation of a secondary structure, which presupposes that the concept specific to the object was already individualized by the formation of the primary structure. The previously individualized concept, which makes us aware of this and ensures that we continue to observe *this* specific object, searches, with increasing certainty and clarity, for the perceptible elements assigned within its structural scope. Through this assignment these elements are generalized (universalized): *Each one* of them belongs to the same area through diverse (universal) relations, they are *all* equal to each other in this interweaving (though in specific ways), they are apprehended and organized within the appropriate region of *a particular* individualization. The structuring concept, which is already individualized, universalizes itself by individualizing what is already universalized. Here a process occurs in which the formative activities and the nature of the elements that they apprehend are reversed in respect to the formation of the basic structure. Therefore, this process corresponds exactly to the construction process of the memory structure. The previously individualized concept (e.g., *this* glass, *this* tree) corresponds to the recollective disposition of a supposed remembering; for this concept gives confirmation of what is already known. Certainly, its character of being already known is vague, in a manner that can only arise from a subconscious process. However, it indeed effects our observation and determines its subsequent character in relation to the preceding basic structure. When we observe a tree in a normal mindset, we do not reach the moment in which the basic structure arises. Rather, we are aware of the basic structure itself, though only vaguely. When we observe a tree, we already "know" about the tree (its prior realization), without actually knowing what it is that we know. And we remember this knowledge by retrieving the previously universalized field (which is interwoven with mutually permeating, coherence-forming processes that are variously interlaced with each other) with an individualized intention directed toward its content. The concept's previously individualized intention (*this* glass, *this* tree) is thereby permeated by a dim consciousness of the universality that establishes wholeness in the coherence (a glass *as such*, a tree *as such*); we have prior knowledge of this coherence, which can be universalized, but is not yet individualized. This coherence forms the basis of the intention that is directed toward the secondary layer. In a complementary manner, the previously universalized perceptible elements correspond, with respect to their structural modality, to the dispositional memory traces, which are left in our organism by the formation of the basic structure. That this modality is indeed characteristic of them (i.e., their memory-like deposition on the basic structure) becomes unmistakably clear from the observation of their pre-given relation to the whole. For when we scan the field of an object in observation we always hold the relation of an apprehended element to its whole in our memory. Just as the searching, individually predisposed concept is permeated by a dim consciousness of its universality, so too are the pre-given universally disposed elements tinged with a dim sense of their pure perceptibility.

No thorough self-examination of our objectivity-supposing observational behavior can escape the conclusion that there is a memory layer deposited onto the basic structure. We can convince ourselves of this experimentally with arbitrarily selected pieces of evidence. The insight that it cannot be otherwise can also be attained through observation that penetrates to the basic structure. The peculiar desiring nature of the attitude of consciousness that presumes to grasp presence (but in truth only remembers) becomes conspicuous here, but also understandable. For this type of consciousness, its recollective dispositions have to seek the memory dispositions that they need and therefore demand. Through the memory traces that remain in our organization, our dreaming-remembering mode of representation becomes aware of the sleeping-inhering mode of representation which forms its basis. Our dream desires our sleep in supposed wakefulness. It is the selfish desire for our corporeality, because it is our corporeality that preserves the memory traces. The superficiality is the origin of both selfishness and its superstition that living is the purpose of life.

This yields the *concept of objectivity* and elucidates the origin and nature of the supposition of objective presence. Regarded structurally, objectivity is the memoratively formed representational layer that is deposited onto the basic structure. Its supposed presentification arises through the desire for our corporeality (due to our sensuality). The supposition of an objective presentification wants *only* to receive reality in the form of what is *only* perceptible. It is inert. It is also fearful; for it wants to enjoy and preserve its inherited corporeal possessions instead of daring to walk into the open, into the realm of what cannot be inherited, but rather only acquired Its preference for action over knowing is in truth the concern for the preservation of its own corporeality and uninterrupted enjoyment. The supposition of an objective presentification is, however, right insofar as self-giving excludes, in the same act, the apprehension of the memorative form of objects which it determines. Is there, then, in truth no awareness of *presence*?

Observation must depresentify due to self-giving. That is its law. When it attends to an object, it can only apprehend this as something already temporalized. Due to its evidential capacity it is, however, anchored in the super-temporal. Observation unifies itself with the super-temporal and distinguishes itself from the non-evidential. It participates generatively in the rememberable world that arises out of the sub- and super-temporal. That which is presumed to be stable is illusory, it passes away, because it is only something representationally remembered. What is observed in this way can only relate to what is past. But observation itself is depresentifying because, although it is also temporally determinative and determined, it participates in the duration of the unchanging formation of structure. It arises by actualizing duration, itself in and from duration. This participation in duration remains subconscious as long as it is not apprehended in terms of structure phenomenology. However, this dim consciousness is in essence eternal presence. It is origination from duration, action in duration and self-realization from duration.[5] In frivolous habit, the dim awareness of being a creature of duration reverses into the

---

[5][Bergson, 1912]

blunt desire to receive fixed presence, into sensuousness. In desiring presence one desires one's own body, believing that one thus gains possession of being. By keeping hold of it one seeks to assuage the longing for duration which lives in the creature of duration. This is possessiveness. With the possession of the body one wants to grasp possession of the world instead of generously bringing to the world, in one's own being, what the world itself cannot give one. However, what is observed of the experience of duration as something objectified is always something past. It is something remembered, which the thirst for sensuality together with its illusion desires as something present.

Observation that presumes and desires presence is deceived by the *thirst for sensual deceit* and thus deceives itself. It confuses the fixation of the transformational potential of concepts, which happens through the perceptual stimuli delivered by the body, with constancy. It confuses the universalization of the perceptible with an alien world that determines us and is yet beyond the reach of our own faculties. It confuses self-giving with acquisition and profit. It thus makes itself blind to true duration, the eternally present occurrence of realization from which we originate, in which we participate and which we transform in us. True observation is the spark of duration that glimmers in temporalization, which we can stoke to a bright flame that shines into the super- and sub-temporal. In accord with its nature and truth, observation is called upon and competent to overcome the craving for sensuality and penetrate to the non-sensual origins of everything objective. Our body does not delude us, rather we delude ourselves regarding our body.[6] It has to deceive us if we

---

[6]["The senses do not deceive; it is the judgment that deceives" (Goethe, 1906, p. 135).]

deceive ourselves regarding it; if we employ our faculties for it, instead of using it to give the world in us new content. This we are only able to do if we penetrate to duration in order to animate it in us. The truth of our observation is the unmasking of its self-deception in penetrating to duration—the truth of our thinking is the transformation of duration into freedom.

Structural remembering is indeed related to remembering that refers to an earlier formation of structure performed by the remembering individual. It is only in this relation that the memory structure can be apprehended at all; for remembering that relates to an earlier structure is nothing other than the more or less clear and complete repetition of the deposited memorative part of that structure. It is the repetition of something already remembered. Without the elucidation of this relation the diverse problems related to the occurrence of memory (which have no place within the given framework) cannot be solved. The supposed primary remembering, which in truth repeats something structurally pre-existent, does indeed relate to the structure that contains its specification. But it lacks the lucid consciousness of the nature of its repeating function; for in the remembering that is not accessed by structure phenomenology the repetition of something that is not remembered is presumed.

As we have seen, our habitual consciousness is a multilayered fabric of interfused modes of representation. The representing memory layer is deposited on a constitutive layer. We sleep through this constitutive layer subconsciously, whereas we dream the memory layer because we are not conscious of its representing nature and interpret it as wakefulness craving presence. It is super-wakefulness, which observes the structure-phenomenological findings and sees through the self-deceit, that directs its attention to the reality sleep from which our dream of reality weaves our memory images. But what do we become aware of when we lift the veil of memory? We recognize that our memory dream conceals both the purely perceptible (non-universal) and the purely conceptual (universal) and thus also the process of unification, through which reality arises in the formation of constitutive (inherent) representations. This gaze can be terrifying because the immeasurable opens up before it. Downward, so to speak, yawns the abyss of the purely perceptible, which no expression can express. Upward, as it were, rises the world of universals, whose heights no finite expression can scale. But what does it mean to become aware of this? It is what we ourselves are, human beings who come to know themselves. The sense of being human is at the same time the self-realization of its meaning. This can only be grasped in the fact that the structure-forming processes continue to the emergence of human organization, in which they then annul themselves. This is how the prerequisite is achieved for the processes that form reality to be continued by a self-creating being. This deworlding of the world takes place in the human organization. The worlding of the deworlded world is the arising of the human spiritual form out of the non-spiritual through the apprehension of universals. This form emerges as does the butterfly from the chrysalis of its organization, which it casts aside. Structure-phenomenology's gaze behind the veil of memory sees the being which either gives the world its meaning or withholds it by seizing its own meaning or missing it. The gaze into the world is the gaze into the human being, and the gaze into the human being is the gaze into the world. In lifting the veil of memory, one beholds oneself, one who emerges from the emerging.

3.8 The Concept of Presence

In order to give this topic extensive attention, let us again pose the question as to whether we do not indeed have true experience of what we usually take to be *present*. One is inclined to insist that the present and the experience of it *must* exist. Yet they *cannot* exist in the form that is desired by the habitual presumption of objective presence; they cannot exist as something present-at-hand without our epistemic participation in the manner of a stockpile, which anyone is able to access and consume at will. The presence of remembering will indeed be persistently asserted and postulated, independent of its content. But let there be no mistake regarding the fact that in the sense of self-giving (which as a result of the basic structure can be stated as a law) one can apprehend neither presence in general, as naïvely demanded, nor the presence of remembering in particular. The presumed presence of remembering, to the extent that it is apprehended as objectively observed and recognized, is itself, due to self-giving, a remembering and not a presence. Presence cannot be reached in this way. Rather, this attempt leads to an infinite regress.

It could be claimed that simultaneous events (such as the arrival of a train and a particular position of the hands of a clock) objectively prove the presence of the events in their relation to each other independently of us. Then, however, both events have already been interpreted as being present, according to our habitual manner. Thus, what is purportedly explained was already presupposed. In addition, something observed is extrapolated to something that may be unobserved. Despite this difficulty, however, it is possible to speak of presence from the perspective of structure phenomenology and legitimize the unexamined desire for presence.

This is because the confluence of the dispositions, whose unification founds the recollectively formed objectivity, has a distinguishing and illuminating characteristic with respect to presence. This characteristic must, however, be protected from misinterpretation in which it would again be lost; for as soon as this unification has occurred and is apprehended as such, remembering (memoratively formed objectivity) has also occurred. What is supposed to be apprehended as present has then already vanished. Nevertheless, the confluence of dispositions that are the structural components of the memorative deposition on the basic structure can and must be conceived of as indicative of presence. They mediate an undoubted sensation and assurance of presence. However, as soon as these dispositions are determined as objective (i.e., when the perceptible, non-universal component is universalized, unified with its concept), they are already remembered and no longer present. This again leads to a self-annulling regress.

This results in something that at first seems paradoxical. Specifically, it follows that presence can be neither reached nor understood at all from the side of objectivity, as is confirmed by careful introspective observation. Presence does not disclose itself to our desire for percept-like consumable objectivity. Reality is not a charitable reward for inactivity. It does not favor consumption, but rather production. To break through to reality demands abstaining from objectness and the body by which it is mediated.[7] If one wants to reach this goal, one must demand of oneself this eschewal. Only from the other side, from the side of our active participation in the emergence of the

---

[7] [This demarcates Witzenmann's approach from Merleau-Ponty's phenomenology of the body which tends to blur the functional boundaries between mental and bodily phenomena (Merleau-Ponty, 2014).]

basic structure, can presence be apprehended and understood. It is the result of our total unification with the evidential and our total differentiation from the non-evidential. These experiences of our activity leave traces in the form of our dispositions. These traces are the result of our participation in the eternal presence of the process of reality, which, as something not itself object-like, precedes all forms of objectivity.[8] What we wishfully suppose as objective presence, thus withdrawing ourselves from it and enshrouding it, manifests itself to our eschewal as our participation in the eternal presence. This presence is of something not objectively apprehensible, but rather only in process; our dispositions are an offshoot of it. Presence, which is attested in us, is the confluence of our dispositions as offshoots of processual non-objectivity, and not as an objective result.

The same also applies to the act with which we perform the unification of the dispositions. As an objective apprehension, this act, too, has a memorative form. In it, too, only the eternal presence is present. In it, too, the degree of presence represents an offshoot of the non-presence in the dispositions from which its memoratively formed objectivity arises.

The offshoots of the non-objective in the dispositions of recollection and memory are true testimony to the presence that forms the basis of the merely presumed and self-deceitful presence of objects. The presence of the memoratively formed objective cannot be reached from the side of its own objectivity, but only from the side of the non- or pre-objective. The metaphors pertaining to our existence can only be illuminating via asceticism. For our awareness, that which is

---

[8][Whitehead, 1929]

truly present, the trace of the experience of duration in the productive and receptive part of our nature, is veiled by our desire for sensuality. The craving for the inactive enjoyment of lingering famishes on the presumptive sips from the chalice of self-deception. The naïve realistic "there is" has to be thoroughly revised and the impossibility of satisfying it with habitual spatial-temporal representation must be recognized. In addition, the unrealistic consumption of reality must be transformed by the testimony of the production of reality. This must be done in the sense of a modern vow of poverty, chastity, and obedience; a poverty that abstains from possession of presence, chastity instead of desiring this possession and obedience as the consequence of self-giving.

In this context a particular doubt must be addressed. The suspicion that the results on which structure phenomenology is based are of a subjective nature becomes stronger the less they account for habit and its persistence. It has already been demonstrated that participation in the basic structure is not subjective, but rather goes beyond its own subjectivity. For in apprehending evidential content, the subjective act experiences its reciprocal determination from the super-subjective and super-objective spiritual coherence. This act assimilates its content-related determination (the immutability of the coherence that it brings forth) into itself without sacrificing its own identity. Rather this is expressed to the spiritual realm inasmuch as this realm is no longer solely universal when it is actualized, but rather also individual.

Yet another suspicion of subjectivity, however, seems possible. It concerns processuality as eternal presence, as the process of ceaseless formation of structure. As structure phenomenology takes this as its starting point, this suspicion seems all the more capable of bringing its claim of validity into question. The decomposing activity of the human organization is a determining factor of structure phenomenology's line of questioning. If the recomposition of this decomposition provides reality with its validity and its content of generative knowing, then the achievement of this reunion seems to be a subjective human affair. Moreover, the processuality of a reality independent of human knowing seems to be challenged by the very assertions of structure phenomenology itself; for it finds its starting point in the evidential and non-evidential, that is in the non-objective and non-temporal. Hence, everything processual seems then to be tainted with a subjective character.

As already mentioned, the present context does not provide the necessary space to explore the multifaceted and extensive problems related to time and movement. They constitute a broad field of research for themselves. Nevertheless, the doubt mentioned above must be considered to the extent that it concerns the basis of this treatise.

It cannot, however, be rebutted by a naïve confidence in the belief that change belongs to our continuous experience, that it manifests itself in continuously changing forms the deeper we penetrate into the microstructure of matter (whatever that is supposed to mean). For here the basic structure is always presupposed, irrespective of which characteristics one attributes to its particular product.

The following discussion, however, is correct (it draws on previously mentioned aspects):

1   The evidential and the non-evidential are parts of a whole, which mutually change each other. These changes do,

however, precede those changes occurring in their products (i.e., temporalized objects). The temporalized products are subject to the conditions that result from the influence that these original parts exert on each other. Nevertheless, we only become aware of the temporalized product of the original in a memoratively formed awareness. However, through our experience of the evidential and non-evidential we also have access to the extra-temporal basis of objectivity. We therefore need to form a concept of processuality that determines extra-temporal change. We become aware of these changes as eternal presence. Such an awareness transcends our remembering and its emergence in the direction of its origin. Thus, the processuality of generative knowing does not only find expression in the process of reunification, which is subjectively conditioned by our organization: For in the reunification of what was decomposed we become aware of the super-temporal processuality of the decomposed components.

For us, then, the super-temporal processuality is imbedded in temporal processes. We become aware of it, on the one hand, through suppressing the activity of our organization. On the other hand, it spills over into the formation of the dispositions that we require for remembering. These two are processes that are temporal and at the same time in a super-temporal conditional relationship. In objective representation we let them precede and follow the super-temporal, which, despite the fact that it is embedded in the temporal, is nevertheless experienced as eternal presence.

2   Further, it could be shown that the formation of reality and beings stand in a relation of mutual determination. The constitutional differentiation of mutual influence that the evidential and non-evidential exert on each other comes to expression in this context. Every being is subject to the same condition, which can be apprehended as the formation of reality in a sequence of conditions. The formation of reality appears, in turn, under the respectively graded conditions of the formation of the beings. We are concerned here with characteristics of the basic structure, whose peculiar nature must not be confused with those that occur in natural evolution (in whatever form this may be). Every result of natural evolution rests on the same structural conditions whose partial conditions in turn mutually condition each other. For the formation of reality and beings it is therefore necessary to form a structural concept of an extra-temporal process that runs out in temporalization.

3   Let us now turn to another characteristic which shows especially strikingly the processuality of the basic process from the reverse. This characteristic becomes apparent specifically when it is considered that the extra-temporal process runs out in temporalization. This temporalization is subjective insofar as the temporalized products are represented after the epistemic recomposition as memory-like objects. The basis of this representation, however, is formed by the conditional relation between the evidential and the non-evidential, whose individual phases are, in turn, connected to one another via conditional relations that take

the form of sub- and superordinate dependencies, that is they are connected processually, though extra-temporally. It is precisely the integration of this process into the human co-creative knowing that allows for a deeper understanding of super-temporal processuality. For the manner in which it happens explains itself through its transition into human knowing. The universal processuality appears as orientated in meaning toward individual processuality. In individual processuality universal processuality attains an entirely new quality of freedom. It is this orientation in meaning toward something new that renders the eternally present processuality completely understandable. The emergence of the human being from processuality makes sense because processuality arises anew in passing through human self-giving. This is the true "universal theory."

It is, therefore, necessary to develop a concept of super-temporal processuality that emerges from temporalization with a new quality. The relations that we must ascribe to extra-temporality and temporality may seem tedious and cumbersome to our habitual nature. In view of the forbearance with which the intellectual challenges of modern quantum mechanics and field theory are accepted, it should also be possible to summon the patience for a far less demanding and more socially relevant intellectual undertaking, even if it does not exhibit as many astonishing relations.

Presence can only be understood as the presence of a universal, extra-temporal process.[9] Presence is an eternally present,

---

[9][Gebser, 1986]

pre-objective process. We can only become aware of it because of the combination of the two modes of observation which already had to be demanded at the introduction of the basic difficulty to its solution. We continually make use of these two modes of observation in our worldly dealings without taking this into account. Our impression of presence is a result of their combination. We can become conscious of their subconscious basis in terms of structure phenomenology. The remembering that presumes and desires presence results from the combination of objective and pre-objective observation. Penetration of the memory veil arrives at the truth of eternal presence behind this deception. The ambivalently frail and yet seemingly assured always-present presence can only be revealed to be eternal presence, which is the past, because it is prior to all temporalization, and the future, because it extends beyond everything already temporalized.

3.9 Structural and Functional Remembering

Only structure-phenomenological research can solve the *problem of memory*. The distinction between object- and process-oriented observation is indispensable for the solution, and most of all, the demonstration that the second mode of observation is possible at all. These are results of the application of the structure-phenomenological method. From this distinction follows the further distinction of a primary *structural* remembering and a secondary *functional* remembering, of which the latter accounts for the autonomous aspect of remembering. The discovery of the conditional relation in which the two forms of memory stand to each other is of fundamental importance for research into memory. This is only able to arrive at valid findings after first deciphering objectivity. Objective representation is, in truth, (structurally primary) remembering, which is repeated (more or less accurately) in functional (secondary) remembering. Secondary memory representations are repetitions of primary memory representations, which are conditioned by acts that cannot be represented as related to objectivity. Secondary remembering relates, therefore, to the basic structure via primary remembering. Functional remembering remembers structural remembering, which, in turn, remembers the basic structure. Structural remembering is the indispensable condition for functional remembering, which is not possible at all without it. This insight, however, can only be gained by first solving the paradox of self-giving and rectifying naïve realism via authentic awareness of the overlapping layers that comprise our contact with reality.

Though this stratification does not lead us into an infinite regress, it should nevertheless be evident from this presentation that structural remembering is in turn deposited upon functional remembering when observation turns to the latter. This secondary structural remembering is, however, simply an indication of the relation between primary structural and functional remembering. The meditative penetration through the memory veil to an awareness of the basic structure has therapeutic implications. For overcoming self-deception restores our lost concord with ourselves and the world.

3.10 The Paradox of Self-giving. The Self-forgetfulness of Supposing

Self-giving requires that its product has a memorative form whilst at the same time excluding the apprehension of this form as such. This is the *paradox of self-giving*: It gives us what we cannot receive. For the product of a process (or a particular successful instance) of self-giving must include a memorative reference. But for its part this reference cannot contain that to which it refers. Although this is banal, it is nevertheless clear that the memorative reference contained within the product cannot be properly understood as long as its correlate remains subconscious, as is habitually the case. A mistaken interpretation is unavoidable under this presupposition. Uncovering the mistake requires unaccustomed effort. The unresolved paradox of self-giving leads to the contradiction between habitual consciousness and the formation of the basic structure.

Reference to something no longer objectively present to hand takes place in all remembering. It can refer only to a structure that was previously present at hand (apprehended, formed). It is only because at any given time we experience the primary formed structures that we can apprehend the secondary memorative reference as such. We thus obtain the possibility of comparison. In what is remembered we can ascertain a similarity (though it is very indeterminate in our habitual behavior) to what appears in the non-remembered, primary structure. This possibility of comparison is among the indispensable items in the toolkit of our consciousness. One of the main tasks of this treatise is to investigate the nature of this similarity. If we did not possess this capacity to compare, we would not be able to distinguish memories from fantasies. Memorative inclusions in fantasies are also subject to this comparison. Correspondingly, we could not accurately characterize the particular nature of structural remembering if we were unable to decode the reference, which it does indeed display, through knowledge of its correlate. This knowledge can only be attained through a specific act that is independent of the result of self-giving. As this has to do with predominately subconscious processes, the mistaken interpretation, which presumes objective presence to have a non-memorative form, can arise as long as these processes are not brought to consciousness.

Therefore, if we have at our disposal a mode of observation that is only oriented toward the objective product of formation, then this product cannot be recognized as such, namely as having a memorative form. With respect to self-giving, in addition to observation of the product, another kind of observation is needed, namely a *mode of observation that is not oriented towards products*. An awareness oriented toward objects can only be understood with recourse to an awareness that is orientated toward processes. However, the exact determination of the significance of the process remains open for this postulate. Nevertheless, only by means of a mode of observation that is not orientated toward product can self-giving be apprehended as a process. And only in this manner is it possible to decode the reference by which the result is characterized as having a memorative form. The combination of both these modes of observation reveals that the supposed non-memorative form of objective presence is a mistaken interpretation.

The discovery of this mistake is difficult because it requires observation of the non-objective. Though we live continually with and within the non-objective we have no knowledge of it unless we follow the path of structure phenomenology. For we are not accustomed to remember our lived experience, but rather to forget it. Reality is not representable in our habitual temporal-spatial objectifications. Nevertheless, reality is by no means unreachable for a form of cognition that detaches itself from these rigid habits of representing. Rather, super-temporal, super-objective, and super-representational awareness leads to an experience of reality on the basis of which objectivity can be interpreted correctly for the first time. The correct interpretation hears the eternal present, the *basso continuo* of the temporalized over which the veil of memory wafts.

3.11 Results of the Structure-Phenomenological Exploration of the Contents of Consciousness

It follows from the above discussion that *objective awareness of objects* is a later, half-conscious result of the earlier subconscious generative process of the basic structure. (The result is half-conscious because its formation has not been consciously inspected.) What is here earlier is later for the awakening introspective observation, which proceeds from what is now earlier and supposedly present to its precondition, and thus to its memorative form which is now later. By shedding its sensual captivity, objective awareness becomes conscious of the memorative form of objects. The depositing effect on the basic structure is to be expected if the basic structure has this generative character. Conversely, as the deposited structure has a memorative form, the generative form of the basic structure is to be expected. The memory structures (and thus the phenomenology of remembering) assume general relevance insofar as they grant access to the basic structures.

It was possible to overcome doubts in connection with *structural temporality* by stating the propositions about structures in terms of super- and sub-temporal elements. As a result, the law of depresentification for observation could be interpreted correctly by demonstrating the interrelations of the various forms of representation (i.e., structurally inherent representations, memoratively representing representations and presumptively presentifying representations).

In addition, the purported slip into an *infinite regress* in the awareness of remembering, which, due to the structurally generative character of remembering, seemed to threaten, could be averted by showing that judgments about memory that themselves are unaffected by memory can be made by means of sub- and super-temporal carriers of meaning.

Further, the *non-presence of the represented*, which belongs to remembering, is ensured in the depositing effect insofar as this effect, similar to remembering presumed as such, reveals itself in pre-deposited connections—which lead to the mistaken conception of the Gestalt theory of perception. The naïve, superficial awareness is the search for a pre-awareness of the basic structure in its absence, though it is only a dim consciousness; this absence is structurally pre-given and thus "presentified" in reciprocal connections. In this respect, the deposit has a deep relation to something prior.

Memory as a representational layer covering the phenomena is possible and necessary (and thus also structure-phenomenological research) because a trace of the primal process remains in the human dispositions and because a reciprocal process in relation to the primal process develops from these dispositions.

Structure-phenomenological research into the contents of consciousness leads, among others, to three important results: Firstly, it gives an answer to the question: In what way can that which is itself not observed in what is objectified be remembered? It thus shows the direction in which the *physiological* basis (the memorative dispositions) of the processes of consciousness can be investigated. Secondly, it provides the basis for a theory of representation which is able to provide a core aspect of *psychology*. Thirdly, it shows the point of departure for *pneumatology*, that is the investigation of the spiritual self-construction of the human being in the formation of structure and the extension of this self-formation in free action.

With regard to the *theory of representation*, which cannot be addressed further in this context, let us note that it must consider the specific stratifications of representation mentioned above. The subconscious inherent representations are translated, with the help of representations that are half-conscious because their memorative character has not been recognized, into representations of the presumption of presence and objectivity, into appetitive representations. These can be dissolved in representations that are experimentally formed and fully consciously true to the process of reality.

The old questions of being and becoming receive a new answer from structure phenomenology. It is only possible to speak of being where there are elements that reside with all their variations in self-determination, in the consistency of the unchanging overall coherence. We can convince ourselves that this overall coherence exists, and with it a mode of being that grants the basic structure its persistence, through our reciprocally determined determining in the apprehension of evidence. Becoming exists because the non-evidential and the adaptation of evidence to it both exist. Cognition of becoming in valid propositions exists because being itself speaks about its unification with non-being (the non-evidential). With super-temporal concepts it interprets its temporalization. The basic structure is the valid statement about being and becoming. To suppose, as does *modern physics*[10] (and with it the established natural sciences), that statements about reality can be made without consideration of the basic structure, is to cleave naïvely to the superficial layer of our world. For all the entities that physics apprehends and produces are basic structures already veiled by a superficial layer. In addition, all statements about them make use of such concealing effects. That is, they assume what they believe and purport to explain and

---

[10]Structure Phenomenology seems to have obtained results similar to those of recent developments in *physics*. If physics regards the non-perceptual character of the atomic realm as established—that is, if physics has developed a general field-theory of fundamental particles that excludes spatial-temporal statements about objects—then the concept of reality that finds expression there seems similar to the one sketched here. Notwithstanding the fact that the experimental results of modern physics will force it to develop a radically new conception of the relation between result and process, between form and movement (for which it, however, lacks the necessary epistemological framework), it is important not to overlook the crucial difference between its mode of research and the new conception advanced here. For does it not also represent the non-perceptual in the habits of thought that it purports to have left behind? For the massless singularities of an asymmetric cosmic field, which have their basis only in statistical regularities, are, together with their field, conceived in the sense of a naïvely presumed objectivity, that is, as represented occurrences of a realm that is, when compared to our productive participation in the formation of structure, of a wholly different nature and only operatively conceivable for us by recourse to a system of mathematical symbols. Contemporary physics does indeed regard the distinction between objective and subjective as problematic, but it does so not because it admits that the only epistemologically tenable conception of reality is that of productive knowing (in its relation to the craving self-deception of naïvely presuming representation and the metaphor of the structurally superimposed representation), but rather because subjectivity as well as objectivity slip away from it into a naïvely objectified non-objectivity.

thus admit, unbeknownst to themselves, their own impotence. The naïvely superficial statements of a natural physical science therefore cannot lay claim to validity for reality. They are simply the instructions for applying varying procedures within a specific area, whose demarcation, which is prescribed to them, is called a model. But it cannot justify this name not only because it is unknown what the model is a model of, but rather because it must indeed remain unknown (because the objective presupposition of the basic process remains unconscious). The model's relation to reality, though unknown, is unjustly presumed, leading to the destruction of our environment and inner world through objectives that are necessarily false; with increasing horror, we are becoming aware of this, without knowing the true cause. Thanks only to our ability to attain evidence for universals can we find a fixed point within the relentlessly surging flow of change; from this standpoint, without being swept along with the stream, we can determine the guidelines for our existence. Only this can vouch for our ability to apprehend reality. The adaptability of being to non-being affords us the capacity to make judgments whose validity is indubitable because it is not temporally determined, but nevertheless appropriate to the temporal. For the temporal is itself one of the dimensions of the validity of these judgments. This validity, which is grounded in the immutable, shows itself in a new existential form as it passes through the human being. This new existential form of the ideational can indeed become grounded in the composition of reality in such a way that the arising of the preconditions for a spiritual humanity takes effect as the driving force of the formational processes. This becomes apparent to structure-phenomenological observation. Reality cannot attain its new existential form by itself, but rather only in passing through and thus by means of the human being. Only insofar as human beings unfold their potential for self-realization themselves can they make new reality arise through the realization of their humanity.[11] This alone is the purpose that we can realize. It is, however, fully sufficient, for it is who we ourselves are.

The structural characterization of objective awareness and also self-awareness is an essential outcome of structure phenomenology. This would not have been possible without the analysis of the memory structure recounted here at least with its main attributes. It is conspicuous that in his book dedicated to the same group of problems, H.-J. Flechtner was in this respect unable to come to a viable characterization of objects and self-awareness and consequently of memory:

> We have already mentioned many times that we are aware of our own *state* …. If the organism is in balance—in the body as well as the psyche—then this state is simply "there". If this balance is… disturbed then our awareness of the state is *noticed* …. Such a disturbance is also observable behaviour, in particular voluntary actions …. This means, however, that this awareness of the body as a whole is particularly intense for haptic perceptions and that it is not lacking for the other senses, but that for them it is simply not, or is only seldom, "noticed". In all perception, our body is affected and involved as a whole, and this whole is stored and retrieved in turn as an *engrammatic state* (Flechtner, 1979, 430ff).

---

[11][See Steiner's philosophy of freedom (Steiner, 1958b) and Maslow's theory of self-actualization (Maslow, 1943).]

It follows from my previous discussion that perceptible wholes neither exist (even as holistic dispositions), nor can exist. It follows further that dispositions cannot be simply retrieved, but must rather be formed during remembering in a process of formation of structure, which is the reenactment of a memorative specification.

The present investigation has outlined the main features of a new epistemological concept, which attains universal importance because, in accordance with its peculiar nature, no subject matter is inaccessible to it and accessibility has been demonstrated by overcoming the difficulties that stand in its way. (This concept is particularly promising in the area of aesthetics and linguistics,[12] where some results have already been achieved and, in combination with what has been developed so far, open up new perspectives.)

Formational stages of being →					Formational stages of reality ←
Percept	Inherence	Meta-morphosis	Intentio-nalization	Actualization	Concept
Area of non-universals	Individualization of the universal and universalization of the non-universal, forming formability, carrier of the memorative deposition	Adaptation of the evidential to the non-evidential, transitional function	Behaviour-specific directing of gaze and orientation, memorative formation deposited on the basic structure, double-disposed, reciprocal to basic structure	Pre-individualization Observation as evidential and non-evidental activity ← → „I' → ←	Area of universals

FIGURE 2 *The Schema of Structure Phenomenology.*

---

[12][For his linguistic concept of ego-morphosis, see Witzenmann, 1987.]

4

The Significance of Structure Phenomenology

Let me append a few remarks on the multidimensional significance of structure phenomenology to this treatise.

The question about *to what end*—that is, the instrumentalizability of human action or behavior in accordance with needs, whether set directly or via the intellectual detour of moral prudence by individuals or the parties they represent—is, though lacking in meaningful justification, the prevalent contemporary attitude; as such, it is advanced as a severe reproach to all others. In contrast, structure phenomenology is the expression of the conviction that the world means to be known; this contribution represents a new approach to cognition in the mode of disclosing. It does not shy from the contempt-filled chalice, which is ready waiting to be poured on its efforts.

Nonetheless, there is no lack of justification of the worth of structure-phenomenological research from particular points of view. The author sees an eminent aspect of its worth in its ability to demonstrate the *subconscious unification* of the human being with the *spiritual formative forces* which occur in all world phenomena as well as in the human being itself as the same type of morphogenesis, though individualizable without limit. Hence, it does not speak of something unknown, but rather of what among all things is best known, of that within which human beings continuously live in ceaseless participation and from which they draw their own spiritual existence. It tells the human being what to do in order to know consciously what is brought about subconsciously and to embrace it as that which can never be received, but rather must always be achieved. In speaking of the spirituality of human beings and the world, structure phenomenology addresses neither credulous subservience nor covetous emotion. It makes no demands other than the sole demand made on its own observation, which continuously monitors itself and is regulated ideationally. Though the gain that it promises is not routinely cheap, it is attainable for the small price of rousing oneself out of intellectual inertia and refusing to employ the full resources of self-conditioning in order to avoid the essential; these states are the titles of honor of the modern human being. Whoever is willing to relinquish these distinctions can, as compensation, look forward to insight into the world and human being.

The fact of generation, which is imbedded in reality as well as in the conception of ourselves, is the guarantor of the *possibility of our freedom*. For surely the solution to the problem of memory uncovers the origin of human freedom, just as it allays the epistemological doubts that can be raised against it. Human beings are not predetermined by a reality that precedes their knowing, but rather can draw from their participation in reality the capacity to bestow on themselves the characteristics of their spiritual existence, which are not typical but rather biographically individual. Thus, acting out of knowledge, they are free in the sense of Rudolf Steiner's *Philosophy of Freedom*.[1]

As a mindset, *materialism* dominates the habits of thought of our time, even where it is rejected for substantive reasons due to sentiment or intellectual considerations. Phenomenologically, scientific materialism can be characterized as the (conscious or unconscious) structural equation of the particular with coherence (individual and universal) such that they are conceived as objectively external to consciousness—often in conjunction with the belief that universals can be either in part or completely explained away. It is irrelevant whether this characterization of the fundamental scientific attitude is recognized as a feature of materialism by its (conscious or subconscious) proponents. For only the demonstration of constitutive and evidential universals in the construction of reality and knowledge is adequate for demonstrating the untenability of the materialistic prejudice. The two most fundamental malaises of our time—alienation from the world and from self—stem from the scientific and materialistic habits of thought and the vulgar variants derived from it. It would require a separate presentation to demonstrate that all these discontents stem from these basic malaises with which modern humanity has infected itself. In principle, however, this should be intelligible to anyone who, even without extensive explanation, has cast a glance into the interlocking of the evidential and the non-evidential. Structure phenomenology is not a new faith based on uncontrolled

---

[1] [Steiner, 1958b]

revelations, but rather a fully conscious path of observation that can be followed by all. This path leads to knowledge both of oneself and of the world as the same kind of spirit-imbued formations.

The *social relevance* of this solidarity through insight can hardly remain hidden from anyone who pursues it. For it is able to do justice to the three things of which humanity is deprived and for which it longs more than anything else, whilst simultaneously striving to maintain its deprivation. They are *meaning, peace,* and *solidarity*.

The dull desire to survive, that is, living for the sake of living, is the *meaninglessness*, whether understood or simply sensed, from which, as a deadly emaciation, present humanity seeks to escape by inoculating itself with it. The demise of present humanity would be preferable to its self-degradation in exclusively pursuing the goal of securing and treasuring its continued material existence (for example in the earthly paradise of a global government). For there is nothing more superfluous and reprehensible than improving or simply maintaining the basis of our material existence if this does not in turn provide the basis upon which humanity can raise its own monument to carry the torch of freedom. The human being has not been prescribed a period of compliant obedience in order to receive a reward, whether in this life or beyond, for good conduct. Rather, with the radical overcoming of all desires that inflate needs, we can determine the goal ourselves in genuine purposeless productivity, namely, to bring our freedom to the spiritual world as an enriching substance which cannot arise without us. The human lot is neither an earthly nor a heavenly reward, it is not a sentimental willingness to help nor one that is well-intended but nevertheless goal-directed, but rather the creative endowment of meaning. No one can impose it upon us, hand it to us or wrest it from us. Only we ourselves can take hold of it and pass it on to the spiritual world. Structure phenomenology is able to impart the insight that there is no other meaning to human existence than that which one embraces for oneself and that this has universal significance.

Structure phenomenology also has the motivation and calling to bring about peace. For it demonstrates that we as human beings can gradually unfold a *peaceable self-generation* in the *meditation-like* practice of becoming aware of our subconscious generative activity. This genuine self-realization is peaceable because it draws on the united and uniting spirit that pervades the human being and the world. The important point here is the gain and loss of self that make up the quotient of true self-realization: self-realization = gain-of-self/loss-of-self.[2]

The *loss of solidarity*, which is muted by the morality of prudence, group egoism, and obedience to authority, the bargaining for prestige, enjoyment, success, and reward are the necessary consequences of a materialistic habit of thought and the concomitant instinct, both of which deny the human capacity for reality and selfhood and thus spiritual humanity altogether. For if human beings are not capable of an inalienable self-determination, but rather are only minute, though complex cogwheels in the mechanism of reality, then they can experience themselves and exist only as beings that gather for

---

[2] The gain-of-self (the becoming aware and free development of our generative participation in the spiritual structuring of reality) and loss-of-self (the spiritually inactive persistence in the busily languid desire of one's own corporality) are not quantities of the same kind whose relation could be shown by subtraction. Rather, they are qualitatively different, coexisting and holistically correlated states. That the numerator approaches infinity as the denominator approaches zero is not absurd, for such an unattainable state would be of infinite value.

themselves reinforcements so that they can better withstand the pressure of reality. By contrast, a line of research such as structure phenomenology, which can account for the human being's original capacity and vocation to create, will additionally impart the conviction that human beings, with respect to their true humanity, can attain nothing through reception, even were they to win the whole world, but only through action. This becomes a virtue of giving, a sense of living in which humans apprehend themselves not as receptive beings, but as thoroughly productive beings—as a self-begetting apprehension of oneself that devotes itself to the community not in the expectation of receiving in return but in the productive joy of participating in the process of community building. This process can in essence be none other than one of performance and response looking upward to the spiritual world.

Structure phenomenology renders conscious our subconscious participation in the *spirituality and spiritual constitution* of the world. It is a protest against the intellectual inertia that (directly or indirectly) serves specific purposes and self-interests and is the cure to this obsession.

The common decision today to grant priority to action over knowledge is fundamentally an ideological (philosophical) one. For it decides on our being-in-the-world and pretends and promises to determine its meaning. In reality, however, it denies the sole meaning embedded within our selfhood. It is equivalent to the practiced doctrine that our task is the preservation of our body rather than the unfolding of our spirit. It is thus the destruction of the inner world and the environment. Experience teaches us that this is the case wherever the decision is made in favor of action (i.e., nowadays worldwide). To understand that this not only *happens* to be so where cognition is misapprehend and even denied, but that it *must* be so, should be regarded as one of the most important requirements of self-scrutiny. For where the penetrating gaze into the structural depths is lacking, all that remains is pre-individualized intentions, which crave to be satiated by bodily dispositions and necessarily seek continual replenishment of this sustenance. If one wants to dedicate attention and support to the fundamental challenge of our time (i.e., the overcoming of egotism), one must demand a certain level of education of oneself. This includes the insight into both the structural basis of the body-oriented desire of the epistemophobic mindset and the dire consequences of this mindset. For this insight, it is beyond doubt that reflection on the survival of humanity is superfluous as long as educational goals and supporting institutions do not exist to which survival can be of service. The objection that such philosophical deliberations presuppose survival overlooks the most essential point. It does not realize that the only reason that we are *still* alive is because we are living off the last remains of civilizations that arose from spiritually based cultures, from impulses that were largely unconscious, but instinctively spiritual. Culture is not a child of the economy, rather the economy is a child of culture. This alone is the saving insight. Its scientific justification is of utmost relevance today.

It is a moving poetic experience, but one that nonetheless stands up to scientific rigor, that the world phenomena are shrouded in *remembering* and rise up out of the interfusing forces of the unfathomable sub-temporal and super-temporal realms from whence they came in order to clothe themselves in the garments of human remembrance.

Hovering between awareness and non-awareness, this enshrouding of the process of creation pervades a consciousness that considers itself applicable to reality and in doing so is still suspicious of itself—this is the *metaphor of our existence*. The notion of the deception of the senses, which materialistic science has driven to the ultimate consequences, does not realize that the gossamer with which we cover all things is woven from the primal elements of being. When we follow its threads we discover that under the superficial layer with which we customarily conceal reality from ourselves a view of the fathomless depth of the non-universal and the unscalable heights of the universal opens up before us. The memorable parable of our existence is mixed out of the ingredients of the incomparable. The roots of our being are nourished by the meaning contained in their inexhaustibility that only we can interpret by establishing our spiritual form. The illusory memorative form of what is objectified, which naïve realism takes for reality, is only deception and self-deception when we interpret it as presence. If, however, we understand that illusion is the mode of appearance of the super- and sub-temporal, then it guides us through itself to being. The unreal contents of our consciousness are, properly understood, structurally related representatives of reality. They too are metamorphoses of the primal process. They do not weaken our capacity for apprehending reality for the sake of the permeating idea, but rather are apt to spur on our search for reality.

Among the oldest topics of contemplation belong the questions of the relation between *consciousness* and *reality* as well as the question of change, that is, of *coming to be* and *passing away*. Structure-phenomenological research portrays them in a new and surprising light. The demands and convulsions of the thirst for and doubt about reality that they inseparably involve are given fair judgment in the new conception; the onslaught undertaken from many sides against the extent of reality contained in consciousness is evaded by characterizing the derealized superficial layer of our experience and apprehension as a metamorphosis of both our capacity to apprehend reality and its reality content. Subconsciousness, dreaming and waking, which are intertwined in a supposing that desires objective presence, are interpreted by super-wakefulness as modes of appearance of a single structure-forming process which appears in countless variations. The human being is as much the product of this process as its producer. In free self-realization, we establish a dimension of our being that elevates these two processes, the active as well as the passive. We make ourselves the answer to the question of being and becoming. Only a structure-phenomenological analysis of the problem of generation can render intelligible the fact that human beings can release the generatively epistemic power of their freedom from occurrent reality.

The unity of *freedom and the cosmic order* is the most important and meaningful result of structure phenomenology.

The conception of a world objectified through inhuman causal coercion lies at the root of an *attitude of violence*.

One of the most important tasks of our time is to encounter this tendency at its root. It is the demand to overcome a purely *utilitarian* mode of thinking, that is, the instrumental, operational approach that grants priority to purposes over the agent of the purposes and which, due to its naïve superficiality, itself refuses to penetrate to the depths from which the spiritual substance wells, which unites *meaning*, *peace*, and *solidarity* in itself. The failure to correctly recognize this task is the origin of the mistakes and wrong decisions in the economic and social arena, which will lay waste to our civilization if it does not recognize late in the day that its problems are educational problems. These problems can only be solved with a new spiritual-scientific civilizing impulse. Not everyone must occupy themselves with securing the foundation of a human and humane education. However, such an education must be available to anyone willing to think and its establishment must be accomplished by those who recognize its significance so that others can rely on it.

Structure phenomenology is not unfruitful criticism. It acknowledges the *cultural value of the materialistic mindset*. For it has brought about a previously unknown wakefulness of consciousness. Now that its service is done, however, we need to use the powers of consciousness that have been acquired to gain access to the spirituality of the world in a modern way.

This access is a *Christian* one. For it vouches for the certainty that the world spirit wants to establish a new epoch of creation in the human spirit. Not the name but the insight determines what is Christian.

Advice for the Reader

Readers who are in a hurry expect helpful advice at the beginning of the text. A reader who only seeks information will turn to it first. The fact that it only appears here expresses the author's hope, perhaps an audacious hope, that some of his readers would, rather than seeking to store results, prefer the transformation of consciousness that can be brought about by following his intellectual efforts. But the reader who wants to gain, in the quickest manner possible, insight into the material presented will begin with this synopsis.

This text proceeds from the demonstration that full reality in the multiplicity of its appearances cannot appear as contents of our consciousness without our co-formative contribution. Rather, we construct everything that we consider real by uniting perceptual and conceptual elements. Initially, we perform this unification unconsciously; it can, however, be made conscious It always occurs when we comprehend something that is initially uncomprehended. It therefore cannot be explained or replaced by something else; for it happens anew with each attempt at explanation.

For this reason the unification of perceptual and conceptual elements will, at first, be called the basic structure; for it assumes a quite general significance, which cannot be evaded by recourse to something else. However, this statement alone does not by any means adequately take the presuppositions and consequences of the basic structure into account. It is only possible to judge whether this is worthy of further deliberation if the proposed line of thought is followed.

Let me mention a few results of following these efforts:

1   The true essence of humans is spiritual, that is, related to their activity of thinking. The world is formed by spiritual forces, that is, forces that are related to human thinking.

2   This result of structure phenomenology is significant because it is obtained by no other means than the observation of the epistemic process. It is therefore neither a belief nor a purely intellectual inference, rather it is a genuine insight. Structure phenomenology therefore regards itself as the overcoming of the materialistic conception of the world based on thoughtful observation, not on deliberation.

3   Structure phenomenology is therefore a meditative path of knowing that nevertheless progresses through the logical organization of observations, guiding the spiritual essence of the human being to the spiritual essence of the world. The author sees in this an essential contribution to the overcoming of the present crisis of meaning and its dire consequences.

4   Structure phenomenology shows that the naïve-realistic conception of reality is not in accordance with its nature. Rather, this conception conceals true reality. At the same time,

however, this concealment is the result of our subconscious participation in reality. It is therefore possible to strike a path that leads from naïve realism to awareness of reality. In following this path the reasons for the naïve-realistic misconstrual will become clear.

However, these results can only be obtained if the difficulties that seem to arise from a generative knowing can be overcome. (These difficulties apply in a similar fashion, incidentally, to any form of generation whatsoever—indeed for every type of movement. However, this can only be briefly touched upon in this study.) For generation is already past when its result becomes present. Thus, if we are only able to develop a consciousness that is restricted to this result, then we lack the ability to shed light on its generation. Were this the case, we would also be unable to know anything about the formation of the basic structure. Our naïve-realistic mindset, however, believes that it only encounters objects that pre-exist it without its own activity and that the environment (or world) in which they are situated pre-exists us in the same manner.

However, if we participate generatively in reality by unceasingly (and usually unconsciously) combining perceptual and conceptual elements with each other, then the result of this combination must display a different constitution. The objective result of the formation by the basic structure must be a memorative one; for it is a content of consciousness that is related to something past. However, this relation can only be judged correctly if we can observe not only the result of this process, but also the process itself. Because it mostly takes place subconsciously, we are unaccustomed to observing it. The observation can only take place in an exceptional state. It has been shown in this book that this exceptional state can be attained by any unprejudiced observer. It also shows the particular character of the observations that can be made in this state. Our willingness to develop such an exceptional state determines whether we succeed in looking behind the memory veil with which we customarily conceal true reality.

Structure phenomenology reveals the memorative form of naïve representation. It points out the path that leads toward the basic structure underlying naïve representation. At the same time it explains how the self-deception of naïve consciousness arises. In connection with this it makes our consciousness of presence intelligible. Further, the discovery of structural remembering is a decisive contribution to memory research; for it is only by becoming acquainted with structural remembering that the emergence of our familiar memorative consciousness, which is aware of its relation to the past, will become intelligible (as demonstrated in this text).

The results of structure-phenomenological research mentioned here are especially significant in respect to the relation between consciousness and reality as well as to the possibility of forming judgments that are true to reality (thus the problem of truth).

Structure phenomenology intends to show a new path to reality. In doing so it is guided by the belief that it is able to offer a remedy for the despair wrought by the materialistic deprivation of reality.

BIBLIOGRAPHY

Aurora, S., & Flack, P. (2018). Principles of structural phenomenology: A basic outline and commentary. Acta Structuralica, 1, 151–69.

Baumeister, R. F. (1998). The self. In D. Gilbert, S. Fiske & G. Lindzey (Eds.), Handbook of social psychology (pp. 680–740). Boston, MA: McGraw Hill.

Bennett, M., & Hacker, P. (2003). Philosophical foundations of neuroscience. Oxford: Blackwell.

Bergson, H. (1912). An introduction to metaphysics (T. E. Hulme, Trans.). New York: G. P. Putnam's Sons. (Original work published 1909).

Bhaskar, R. (2008). A realist theory of science. London: Routledge. (Original work published 1975).

Block, N. (1995). On a confusion about a function of consciousness. In N. Block, O. Flanagan & G. Güzeldere (Eds.), The nature of consciousness (pp. 227–87). Cambridge, MA: MIT Press.

Brentano, F. (1995). Descriptive psychology (B. Müller, Trans.). London: Routledge. (Original work published 1982).

Breyer, T., & Gutland, C. (Eds.) (2016). Phenomenology of thinking: Philosophical investigations into the character of cognitive experiences. London: Routledge.

Brockmeier, J. (2015). Beyond the archive: Memory, narrative, and the autobiographical process. Oxford: Oxford University Press.

Brown, S. R. (2005). Structural phenomenology: An empirically based model of consciousness. New York: Peter Lang.

Carruthers, P. (2005). Consciousness: Essays from a higher-order perspective. Oxford: Oxford University Press.

Chapman, R. M., & Bragdon, H. R. (1964). Evoked responses to numerical and non-numerical visual stimuli while problem solving. Nature, 203, 1155–7.

Crane, T. (1992). The nonconceptual contents of experience. In T. Crane (Ed.), The contents of experience: Essays on perception (pp. 136–57). Cambridge: Cambridge University Press.

Crane, T. (2003). The intentional structure of consciousness. In A. Jokic & Q. Smith (Eds.), Consciousness: New philosophical perspectives (pp. 33–56). Oxford: Oxford University Press.

Crane, T. (2004). Mental substances. In A. O'Hear (Ed.), Minds and persons (pp. 229–50). Cambridge: Cambridge University Press.

Crease, R. (1993). The play of nature. Bloomington: Indiana University Press.
Dainton, B. (2008). The phenomenal self. Oxford: Oxford University Press.
Danziger, K. (1980). The history of introspection reconsidered. Journal of the History of the Behavioral Sciences, 16, 241–62.
Dennett, D. C. (2018). The fantasy of first-person science. In S. Wuppuluri & F. A. Doria (Eds.), The map and the territory: Exploring the foundations of science, thought and reality (pp. 455–73). Cham: Springer Nature.
Depraz, N., Varela, F. J., & Vermersch, P. (2003). On becoming aware: A pragmatics of experiencing. Amsterdam: John Benjamins.
Donnellan, K. (1966). Reference and definite descriptions. The Philosophical Review, 77, 281–304.
Doyon, M. (2016). The "As-Structure" of intentional experience in Heidegger and Husserl. In T. Breyer & C. Gutland (Eds.), Phenomenology of thinking: Philosophical investigations into the character of cognitive experiences (pp. 116–33). London: Routledge.
Dreyfus, H. L. (1982). Husserl, intentionality and cognitive science. Cambridge: MIT Press.
Feibleman, J. K. (1954). Theory of integrative levels. British Journal for the Philosophy of Science, 17, 59–66.
Fiebich, A., & Michael, J. (2015). Mental actions and mental agency. Review of Philosophy and Psychology, 6, 683–93.
Flechtner, H. J. (1979). Das Gedächtnis. Ein neues psychophysisches Konzept [Memory. A new psychophysical concept]. Stuttgart: Hirzel.
Fleck, L. (1979). Genesis and development of a scientific fact. Chicago: University of Chicago Press.
Foerster, H. von (2003). Understanding understanding: Essays on cybernetics and cognition. New York: Springer.
Freeman, W. J. (1999). Consciousness, intentionality, and causality. Journal of Consciousness Studies, 6, 143–72.
Gallagher, S., & Schmicking, D. (2010). Handbook of phenomenology and cognitive science. Dordrecht: Springer.
Gebser, J. (1986). The ever-present origin (N. Barstad & A. Mickunas, Trans.). Athens: Ohio University Press. (Original work published 1949).
Gehlen, A. (1988). Man: His nature and his position in the world. New York: Columbia University Press.
Giorgi, A. (2009). The descriptive phenomenological method in psychology. A modified Husserlian approach. Pittsburgh: Duquesne University Press.
Goethe, J. W. (1906). Maxims and reflections (B. Saunders, Trans.). New York: Macmillan. (Original work published 1833).
Goethe, J. W. (1988). Scientific studies (D. Miller, Ed. & Trans.). New York: Suhrkamp. (Original work published 1883–1897).

Goff, P. (2017). Consciousness and fundamental Reality. Oxford: Oxford University Press.
Goodman, N. (1956). A world of individuals. In I. M. Bochenski, A. Church & N. Goodman (Eds.), The problem of universals: A symposium (pp. 13–31). Notre Dame: University of Notre Dame Press.
Gurwitsch, A. (2010). Husserl's theory of the intentionality of consciousness in historical perspective. In J. García-Gómez (Ed.), The collected works of Aron Gurwitsch (1901–1973) (pp. 351–81). Dordrecht: Springer.
Gutland, C. (2018). Husserlian phenomenology as a kind of introspection. Frontiers in Psychology, 9, Art. 896. https//doi.org/10.3389/fpsyg.2018.00896
Hallie, P. (1959). Maine de Biran. Reformer of empiricism. 1766–1824. Cambridge: Harvard University Press.
Hartmann, K. (2010). Herbert Witzemann. Eine Biographie. Teil I (1905–1961). Dornach: Gideon Spicker
Hartmann, K. (2013). Herbert Witzemann. Eine Biographie. Teil II (1962–1988). Dornach: Gideon Spicker.
Hartmann, N. (1964). Der Aufbau der realen Welt. Grundriss der Allgemeinen Kategorienlehre (3rd edn.). [The structure of the real world. Outline of the general theory of categories]. Berlin: De Gruyter.
Heidegger, M. (1962). Being and time (J. Macquarrie & E. Robinson, Trans.). Oxford: Blackwell. (Original work published 1927).
Herder, J. (2002). Treatise on the origin of language (1772). In M. Forster (Ed.), Herder: Philosophical writings (Cambridge Texts in the History of Philosophy, pp. 65–164). Cambridge: Cambridge University Press.
Husserl, E. (1970). The crisis of European sciences and transcendental phenomenology: An introduction to phenomenological philosophy (E. Carr, Trans.). Evanston: Northwestern University Press. (original work published 1954).
Husserl, E. (1973a). Zur Phänomenologie der Intersubjektivität [On the phenomenology of intersubjectivity]. Dritter Teil: 1929–1935. (Vol. XV Husserliana). Den Haag: Martinus Nijhoff.
Husserl, E. (1973b). Experience and judgment: Investigations in a genealogy of logic (J. S. Churchill & K. Ameriks, Trans.). Evanston: Northwestern University Press. (Original work published 1938).
Husserl, E. (1977). Phenomenological psychology (J. Scanlon, Trans.). (Vol. IX Husserliana). Den Haag: Martinus Nijhoff. (Original work published 1962).
Husserl, E. (1980). Ideas pertaining to a pure phenomenology and to a phenomenological philosophy. Third book: Phenomenology and the foundation of the sciences (T. Klein & W. Pohl, Trans.). Den Haag: Martinus Nijhoff. (Original work published 1971).
Husserl, E. (1983). Ideas pertaining to a pure phenomenology and to a phenomenological philosophy. First book: General introduction to a pure

phenomenology (F. Kersten, Trans.). Den Haag: Martinus Nijhoff. (Original work published 1977).

Husserl, E. (1997). Psychological and transcendental phenomenology and the confrontation with Heidegger (1927–1931) (T. Sheehan & R. E. Palmer, Trans. & Eds.). Dordrecht: Springer.

Husserl, E. (2001). Logical investigations. Vol. 2. (J. N. Findlay, Trans., D. Moran, Ed.). London: Routledge. (Original work published 1984).

Jack, A. I., & Roepstoff, A. (2003). Why trust the subject? Journal of Consciousness Studies, 10, V–XX.

James. W. (1912). Essays in radical empiricism. New York: Longman Green & Co.

Kim, J. (2006). Emergence: Core ideas and issues. Synthese, 151(3), 547–59.

Klein, S. B. (2014). Sameness and the self: Philosophical and psychological considerations. Frontiers in Psychology, 5. https://doi.org/10.3389/fpsyg.2014.00029

Kleineberg, M. (2017). Integrative levels. Reviews of Concepts in Knowledge Organization, 44(5), 349–79.

Kockelmans, J., & Kisiel, T. (1970). Phenomenology and the natural sciences. Evanston: Northwestern University Press.

Kriegel, U., & Williford, K. (Eds.) (2006). Self-representational approaches to consciousness. Cambridge: MIT Press.

Laurence, S., & Margolis, E. (2001). The poverty of the stimulus argument. British Journal for the Philosophy of Science, 52, 217–76.

Lieberman, D. A. (1979). Behaviorism and the mind: A (limited) call for a return to introspection. American Psychologist, 34(4), 319–33.

Marsh, H. W., & Craven, R. G. (2006). Reciprocal effects of self-concept and performance from a multidimensional perspective: Beyond seductive pleasure and unidimensional perspectives. Perspectives on Psychological Science, 1(2), 133–63.

Maslow, A. H. (1943). A theory of human motivation. Psychological Review, 50(4), 370–96.

Mathews, F. (2011). Panpsychism as paradigm. In M. Blamauer (Ed.), The mental as fundamental: New perspectives on panpsychism (pp. 141–56). Heusenstamm: Ontos.

Merleau-Ponty, M. (2014). Phenomenology of perception (D. A. Landes, Trans.). London: Routledge. (Original work published 1945).

Meyer, A., Hackert, B., & Weger, U. (2018). Franz Brentano and the beginning of experimental psychology: Implications for the study of psychological phenomena today. Psychological Research, 82, 245–54.

Montero, B. G. (2010). A Russellian response to the structural argument against physicalism. Journal of Consciousness Studies, 17(3/4), 70–83.

Nagasawa, Y., & Wager, K. (2017) Panpsychism and priority cosmopsychism. In G. Gruentrup & L. Jaskolla, (Eds.), Panpsychism: Contemporary perspectives (pp. 113-29). Oxford: Oxford University Press.

Nanay, B. (2015). Perceptual representation/perceptual content. In M. Matthen (Ed.), The Oxford handbook of philosophy of perception (pp. 153-67). Oxford: Oxford University Press.

O'Callaghan, C. (2008). Object perception: Vision and audition. Philosophy Compass, 4(3), 803-29.

Oevermann U. (2016). "Krise und Routine" als analytisches Paradigma in den Sozialwissenschaften ["Crisis and routine" as analytical paradigm in social science]. In R. Becker-Lenz, A. Franzmann, A. Jansen & M. Jung (Eds.), Die Methodenschule der Objektiven Hermeneutik (pp. 43-114). Wiesbaden: Springer VS.

Petitmengin, C., & Bitbol, M. (2013). A defense of introspection from within. Constructivist Foundations, 8(3), 269-79.

Piaget, J., & Inhelder, B. (1969). The psychology of the child New York: Basic Books.

Popper, K. R. (1963). Conjectures and refutations. London: Routledge.

Popper, K. R. (2002). The logic of scientific discovery. London: Routledge.

Powell, J., Lewis, P., Dunbar, R. I., Garcıa-Finana, M., & Roberts, N. (2010). Orbital prefrontal cortex volume correlates with social cognitive competence. Neuropsychologia, 48, 3554-62.

Pylyshyn, Z. (2009). Perception, representation, and the world: The FINST that binds. In D. Dedrick & L. Trick (Eds.), Computation, cognition, and pylyshyn (pp. 3-48). Cambridge: MIT Press.

Quine, W. V. O. (1981). Theories and things. Cambridge: Harvard University Press.

Ramsey, F. P. (1925). Universals. Mind, 34, 401-17.

Reisberg, D., Pearson, D. G., & Kosslyn, S. M. (2003). Intuitions and introspections about imagery: The role of imagery experience in shaping an investigator's theoretical views. Applied Cognitive Psychology, 17, 147-60.

Ribot, T. (1882). Diseases of the memory: An essay in the positive psychology. New York: Appleton & Co.

Robins, S. K. (2016). Misremembering. Philosophical Psychology, 29, 432-47.

Rombach, H. (1971). Strukturontologie: Eine Phänomenologie der Freiheit [Structural ontology: A phenomenology of freedom]. Freiburg: Alber.

Rosenthal, D. (1990). The nature of mind. Oxford: Oxford University Press.

Ross, M. (1995). Soziale Wirklichkeitsbildung. Erkenntnistheoretische, methodologische und anthropologische Grundlagen bei Max Weber und Rudolf Steiner [Social reality formation: Epistemological, methodological, and anthropological foundations in Max Weber and Rudolf Steiner].

Dissertation at the Faculty of Economics and Social Sciences of the University of Dortmund.

Russell, B. (1967). Letter to Frege. In J. van Heijenoort (Ed.), From Frege to Gödel (pp. 124–5). Cambridge: Harvard University Press. (Original work published 1902).

Ryle, G. (2009). The concept of mind (60th anniversary edn.). London: Routledge.

Schaffer, J. (2010). Monism: The Priority of the whole. Philosophical Review, 119(1), 31–76.

Schear, J. K. (Ed.) (2013). Mind, reason, and being-in-the-world: The McDowell-Dreyfus debate. London: Routledge.

Schieren, J. (1998). Anschauende Urteilskraft. Methodische und philosophische Grundlagen von Goethes naturwissenschaftliches Erkennen [Intuitive power of judgment. Methodological and philosophical foundations of Goethe's scientific approach]. Düsseldorf: Parerga.

Schopenhauer, A. (1907). On the will in nature (K. Hillebrand, Trans.). London: Chiswick Press. (Original work published 1836).

Schwitzgebel, E. (2008). The unreliability of naïve introspection. Philosophical Review, 117, 245–73.

Searle, J. (1983). Intentionality. Cambridge: Cambridge University Press.

Shani, I. (2015). Cosmopsychism: A holistic approach to the metaphysics of experience. Philosophical Papers, 44(3), 389–437.

Shapere, D. (1982). The concept of observation in science and philosophy. Philosophy of Science, 49(4), 485–525.

Siewert, C. (2017). Consciousness and intentionality. In E. N. Zalta (Ed.), The Stanford Encyclopedia of Philosophy (Spring 2017 Ed.). https://plato.stanford.edu/archives/spr2017/entries/consciousness-intentionality/

Sinha, D. (1969). Phenomenology as philosophy of science. Dordrecht: Springer.

Skinner, B. F. (1957). Verbal behavior. Acton: Copley Publishing.

Skinner, B. F. (1974). About behaviorism. New York: Vintage.

Smith, D. W., & Thomasson, A. L. (Eds.) (2005). Phenomenology and philosophy of mind. Oxford: Oxford University Press.

Smith, D. W. (2004). Mind world: Essays in phenomenology and ontology. Cambridge: University Press.

Soteriou, M. (2013). The mind's construction: The ontology of mind and mental action. Oxford: Oxford University Press.

Steiner, R. (1958a). Wahrheit und Wissenschaft [Truth and science]. Dornach: Rudolf Steiner.

Steiner, R. (1958b). Die Philosophie der Freiheit. [The philosophy of freedom]. Dornach: Rudolf Steiner Verlag.

Steiner, R. (1972). An outline of occult science (M. Monges & B. Monges, Trans.). Spring Valley: Anthroposophic Press. (Original work published 1910).

Steiner, R. (1975). Letter to F. T. Vischer on "Atomism and its Refutation" (25. Nov. 1886) (R. Hofrichter, Trans.). Spring Valley: Mercury Press.

Steiner, R. (1987). Theosophie. Einführung in übersinnliche Weltanschauung und Menschenbestimmung [Theosophy: An introduction to the supersensible knowledge of the world and the destination of man]. Dornach: Rudolf Steiner.

Steiner, R. (2003). Grundlinien einer Erkenntnistheorie der Goetheschen Weltanschauung [Theory of knowledge implicit in Goethe's world conception]. Dornach: Rudolf Steiner.

Stumpf, C. (1907). Zur Einteilung der Wissenschaften [On the classification of sciences]. Berlin: Verlag der königl. Akademie der Wissenschaften.

Tarski, A. (1983). Logic, semantics, metamathematics: Papers from 1923 to 1938 (2nd edn., J. Corcoran, Ed.), Indianapolis: Hackett Publishing. (Original work published 1956).

Thomasson, A. (2003). Introspection and phenomenological method. Phenomenology and the Cognitive Sciences, 2, 239–54.

Veiga, Marcelo da (2016). Grundmotive im philosophischen Denken Rudolf Steiners und ihr Bezug zu Methoden und Fragestellungen in der Phänomenologie und der analytischen Philosophie [Basic motifs in Rudolf Steiner's philosophical thought and their relation to methods and questions in phenomenology and analytic philosophy]. In J. Schieren (Ed.), Handbuch Waldorfpädagogik und Erziehungswissenschaft. Standortbestimmung und Entwicklungsperspektiven (pp. 82–113). Weinheim: Juventa Beltz.

Wagemann, J. (2010). Gehirn und menschliches Bewusstsein Neuromythos und Strukturphänomenologie [Brain and human consciousness. Neuro-myth and structure phenomenology]. Aachen: Shaker.

Wagemann, J. (2011). The structure-phenomenological concept of brain-consciousness correlation. Mind and Matter, 9(2), 185–204.

Wagemann, J. (2016). Erkenntnisgrundlagen der Waldorfpädagogik [Epistemological foundations of Waldorf education]. In J. Schieren (Ed.), Handbuch Waldorfpädagogik und Erziehungswissenschaft. Standortbestimmung und Entwicklungsperspektiven (pp. 31–82). Weinheim: Juventa Beltz.

Wagemann, J. (2017). Zur Anthropologie der Waldorfpädagogik – Ein bewusstseinseinsphänomenologischer Zugang [On the anthropology of Waldorf education – A consciousness-phenomenological approach]. Research on Steiner Education, 8(1), 1–21.

Wagemann, J. (2018). The confluence of perceiving and thinking in consciousness phenomenology. Frontiers in Psychology, 8, Article 2313. https://doi.org/10.3389/fpsyg.2017.02313

Wagemann, J. (2019). Herbert Witzenmann's path to the philosophical sources of anthroposophy (Part I). Research on Steiner Education, 10(2), 20–8.

Wagemann, J. (2020a). Mental action and emotion – What happens in the mind when the stimulus changes but not the perceptual intention. New Ideas in Psychology, 56. https://doi.org/10.1016/j.newideapsych.2019.100747

Wagemann, J. (2020b). Herbert Witzenmann's path to the philosophical sources of Anthroposophy (Part II). Research on Steiner Education, 11(1), 20–7.

Wagemann, J. (2022a). Exploring the structure of mental action in directed thought. Philosophical Psychology, 35(2), 145–76.

Wagemann, J. (2022b). Voluntary auditory change: First-person access to agentive aspects of attention regulation. Current Psychology. Advance online publication. https://doi.org/10.1007/s12144-021-02662-y

Wagemann, J., Edelhäuser, F., & Weger, U. (2018). Outer and inner dimensions of brain and consciousness – Refining and integrating the phenomenal layers. Advances in Cognitive Psychology, 14, 167–85.

Wagemann, J., & Raggatz, J. (2021). First-Person dimensions of mental agency in visual counting of moving objects. Cognitive Processing, 22(3), 453–73.

Wagemann, J., & Weger, U. (2021). Perceiving the other self. An experimental first-person account of non-verbal social interaction. American Journal of Psychology, 134(4), 441–61.

Waldenfels, B. (2011). Phenomenology of the alien: Basic concepts. Evanston: Northwestern University Press.

Watzl, S. (2017). Structuring mind: The nature of attention and how it shapes consciousness. Oxford: Oxford University Press.

Watzl, S. (2018). Consciousness and no self? Ratio, 3, 363–75.

Weger, U., & Wagemann, J. (2015a). The challenges and opportunities of first-person inquiry in experimental psychology. New Ideas in Psychology, 36, 38–49.

Weger, U., & Wagemann, J. (2015b). The behavioral, experiential and conceptual dimensions of psychological phenomena: Body, soul and spirit. New Ideas in Psychology, 39, 23–33.

Weger, U., Meyer, A., & Wagemann, J. (2016). Exploring the behavioral, experiential, and conceptual dimensions of the self: Introducing a new phenomenological approach. European Psychologist, 21(3), 180–94.

Weger, U., Wagemann, J., & Meyer, A. (2018a). Introspection in psychology: Its contribution to theory and method in memory research. European Psychologist, 23(3), 206–16.

Weger, U., Wagemann, J., & Meyer, A. (2018b). Researching mind wandering from a first-person perspective. Applied Cognitive Psychology, 32(3), 298–306.

Weik, E. (2016). Goethe and the study of life: A comparison with Husserl and Simmel. Continental Philosophy Review, 50, 335–57.

Weizsäcker, V. von (1986). Der Gestaltkreis. Theorie der Einheit von Wahrnehmen und Bewegen [The Gestalt-circle. Theory of unity of perception and movement] (6th edn.). Stuttgart, Germany: Thieme.

Wettig, S. (2009). Imagination im Erkenntnisprozess. Chancen und Herausforderungen im Zeitalter der Bildmedien [Imagination in the cognitive process. Opportunities and challenges in the age of visual media]. Bielefeld: Transcript.

Whitehead, A. N. (1929). Process and reality: An essay in cosmology. New York: Macmillan.

Wittgenstein, L. (1999). Tractatus logico-philosophicus. Mineola: Dover.

Witzenmann, H. (1977). Intuition und Beobachtung [Intuition and observation]. Vol. I. Stuttgart: Freies Geistesleben.

Witzenmann, H. (1978). Intuition und Beobachtung [Intuition and observation]. Vol. II. Stuttgart: Freies Geistesleben.

Witzenmann, H. (1983a). Strukturphänomenologie. Vorbewusstes Gestaltbilden im erkennenden Wirklichkeitenthüllen. Ein neues wissenschaftstheoretisches Konzept im Anschluss an die Erkenntniswissenschaft Rudolf Steiners [Structure phenomenology. Preconscious formation in the epistemic disclosure of reality. A new concept of philosophy of science based on Rudolf Steiners's epistemology]. Dornach: Gideon Spicker.

Witzenmann, H. (1983b). Strukturphänomenologie. Ein neues wissenschaftstheoretisches Konzept [Structure phenomenology. A new epistemological concept]. Beiträge zur Weltlage, 69, 3–27.

Witzenmann, H. (1984a). Strukturphänomenologie. Grundgedanken zu einer wirklichkeitserfassenden Erkenntniswissenschaft [Structure phenomenology: Basic thoughts on a reality-apprehending epistemology]. Die Drei, 5, 3–27.

Witzenmann, H. (1984b). Vom vierfachen Quell lebendiger Rechts [On the fourfold origin of lively right]. Dornach: Gideon Spicker

Witzenmann, H. (1985). Stoff und Form. [Matter and Form]. In H. Witzenmann (Ed.), Beppe Assenza (1st edn. 1978) (pp. 105–29). Stuttgart: Freies Geistesleben.

Witzenmann, H. (1986). Die Voraussetzungslosigkeit der Anthroposophie [The unconditionality of Anthroposophy]. Stuttgart: Freies Geistesleben.

Witzenmann, H. (1987). Goethes universalästhetischer Impuls [Goethe's universal aesthetic impulse]. Dornach: Gideon-Spicker-Verlag.

Witzenmann, H. (1989a). Sinn und Sein [Sense and being]. Stuttgart: Freies Geistesleben.

Witzenmann, H. (1989b). Evolution und Struktur [Evolution and structure]. In W. A. Arnold (Ed.), Entwicklung. Interdisziplinäre Aspekte zur Evolutionsfrage [Development. Interdisciplinary aspects of the evolution question] (pp. 9–26). Stuttgart: Urachhaus.

Witzenmann, H. (1989c). Was ist Meditation? [What is meditation?] (2nd edn.). Dornach: Gideon Spicker.

Witzenmann, H. (1994). Die Kategorienlehre Rudolf Steiners [Rudolf Steiner's category theory]. Krefeld: Gideon Spicker.

Witzenmann, H. (2005). Hegel, der Philosoph der Goetheschen Weltanschauung [Hegel, the philosopher of Goethe's world view]. Beiträge zur Weltlage, 152(1), 5-20.

Zahavi, D. (2003). Husserl's phenomenology. Stanford: Stanford University Press.

INDEX

abstraction xii–xiii, xlii
  theory 13–14, 20, 37
access xx, xxiv, xxxii, xxxix, l, liv, 63, 68, 76, 92
act xxviii, 12, 23, 27, 31–2, 34, 45–8, 59, 65–6, 74
action 19, 59, 77, 83, 88
activity ix, xxv, xxvii–xxxi, xxxv, xxxvii, lvi, 8–9, 19, 24, 34, 36, 38–9, 43, 47–50, 53, 65, 67–8, 87, 95
actuality xxv, xxix, xl, 48
  actualized xxviii, xxxv, 35–6, 38, 41–2, 47, 66
adaptation xli, 36–7, 39, 44, 78
affection 6, 18
  theory lix, 5–6, 12, 20
alien xxxi–xxxii, 9, 60, 85
anthroposophy xv–xvi
attention xlix, lii, 1, 6, 47, 52
  direction of ix, xix, xxvi, xxxiv, 45, 47–8, 62
Aurora, S. liv
autonomous xlviii, 15, 71
  observation xxix, 19
awareness xxi, 11, 25, 28, 33–4, 44–6, 50, 54–6, 59, 65, 68, 72, 74–6, 80, 90, 95

basic structure xxii, xxv, xxvii–xxviii, xxxi–xxxviii, xl, xlii, l–li, lv–lvi, 3, 5, 7, 9, 11–13, 15, 17–28, 42–3, 45–6, 48–50, 52–8, 63–7, 69, 72–3, 75–8, 93–6

being xxxix, xlii–xliii, xlv, 9, 21, 24, 41, 43–4, 46, 57, 59–60, 62–3, 69, 77–9, 88, 90–1
Bergson, H. 25, 59
Berkeley, G. xliii
Bhaskar, R. 7
Biran, F. P. G. Maine de xlvi
body xlv, 60, 64, 80, 88–9
  bodily xxxv, xxxvii, 89
Brentano, F. xii, xiv, xxii, xxvi
Brown, S. R. liv

causal xlv, 6, 91
Chapman, R. M. 15
Chomsky, N. xxxi
cognition xxxiii, xliv, 8, 18, 27, 37, 42–3, 75, 78, 83, 89
coherence xviii, xx, xxvii, xxxv, xlii, xliv–xlvii, 9, 11–12, 14–15, 31–2, 40, 46–7, 53, 55, 57, 66, 77, 85
  coherent xxxv, xl, 31
complementary xx, xxvii, xxxi–xxxii, xxxv–xxxvi, xl, xliii, 45, 51, 57
component xxxii–xxxiii, xxxv, 8, 11, 15, 20, 53, 64, 68
concept xx, xxii, xxv, xxviii, xxxv, xxxvii, xxxix, xl–xli, xlv, xlvii–xlviii, lii, lx, 5, 9–12, 14, 17–18, 20–2, 26, 31–42, 44–8, 51, 54–8, 60, 63–4, 68–70, 78, 81
  conceptual xvii–xx, xxv–xxxv, xxxvii–xxxviii, xl–xli, xliii,

lv, 9–15, 20, 22, 28–9, 32, 34, 37–9, 42, 44–7, 49, 51, 53, 62, 93, 95
condition xxvi, xliii, li, 12, 18, 45, 69, 72
consciousness xiv–xv, xvii–xviii, xx–xxiv, xxviii, xxxvi–xxxvii, xxxix–xl, xliii–xliv, xlvii–xlviii, li, lv, lix–lx, 5–6, 10, 16, 18, 33, 36, 46, 48, 54–9, 61, 73–7, 85, 90–3, 95–6
constitution xxii–xxiv, xxxiv–xxxv, xxxvii, 12, 19, 23, 28, 42–3, 88, 95
  constitutive xiv, xxiv, xxix, xxxii, xxxix, xli, xlvi, 43, 55, 61–2, 85
construction xii, xliv, lx, 6, 11, 13, 19, 22, 28, 34, 38, 40–1, 44, 49, 51–3, 56, 77, 85
cosmopsychism xlvii, xlix
cosmos xlvii–xlviii
  cosmic xlvii–xlviii, 91
Crane, T. xlvii
creation 43, 90, 92

deceit/deception 29, 60–2, 65–6, 71–2, 78, 90, 96
decomposition xxxv–xxxvi, xliii, xlvi, xlviii, 29, 49, 67
deductive 2, 17
deposition xxxv, 57, 64
  deposited xv, xxxii, xxxiv, xxxvii, l, 54–5, 58, 61, 72, 75
depresentification 18, 27, 45, 59, 76
derivative xxxii, xxxvi, 55
Dilthey, W. 2
disposition xxxv–xxxvii, l, 49–52, 56–8, 64–5, 68, 77, 81, 89
  disposed 53, 58
dream 58, 61–2
Dreyfus, H. xxviii
duration 21, 59–61, 66

element xxxii–xxxv, xli, xliii, 8–14, 16, 20–3, 28–9, 32–5, 37, 39–53, 55–8, 76–7, 90, 93, 95
epistemology xii, xiv, xvi, l, 9
essence 41, 59, 88, 94
eternal 59–60, 65–6, 68, 70–1, 75
evidence xxvi, lix–lx, 31–5, 38, 40–3, 45, 47–8, 50, 58, 78–9
  evidential xxv–xxxi, 33, 36, 39–41, 45, 47–8, 59, 65–9, 85
evolution xliv–xlvi, 69
exceptional state xix, li, 41, 54–5, 96
experience xii–xiii, xvii–xx, xxii–xxvi, xxxii–xxxiii, xxxvii, xxxix, xlii, li, lv–lvi, 7, 36, 47, 51, 55, 60, 63, 66–8, 73, 75, 87–9, 91
experimental xiii, xxi, lii, liii, lvi, 61, 78
eye-opening xviii, xx

first-person xiv, xix, xxiii, xxxi, xxxix, xlii, xlvi, xlviii, lii, lv–lvi
Flack, P. liv
Fleck, L. xviii
Foerster, H. von xxxi
formation xxv–xxvi, xxxviii, xl, 11–12, 14, 18, 21–4, 26, 34–5, 38, 40–6, 49–51, 53–4, 56–7, 59, 61–2, 66, 68–9, 73–5, 77, 81, 95
  of structure xl, 21, 23, 34–5, 40, 42, 44–5, 50–1, 59, 61, 66, 77–8, 81
freedom xlv, 43, 61, 70, 77, 80, 84–7, 91

gaze 54, 62, 89
  gaze-direction xix, xxxii, 10
Gebser, J. 70
generation 2, 12–13, 17, 19, 21, 24–5, 27–9, 31, 33, 46, 54, 84, 87, 91, 95

Gestalt xix, xxxviii, 2, 12–13, 76
Goethe, J. W. von xv, xlvi, 2, 36, 60
Goodman, N. 1
gradual xli, 52
Gutland, C. xviii

Hegel, G. W. F. xlvi
Heidegger, M. xii, xxxix, liv, 18
heteronomous xxix, xxx, 15, 19
homogeneity 15
   homogenous 13
   theory 8–9, 20, 37
human xiv, xxxiii, xliii, xliv–xlv, xlvii, lix–lx, 6–8, 10, 12, 15, 32, 43, 47, 62, 67, 70, 76, 83, 84, 86–7, 89, 92, 94
   being xlii, xlv, lix, 5, 9, 41, 43–4, 62, 70, 77, 79–80, 84, 68–8, 94
   organization 7, 62, 67
humanity 79–80, 85–9
Husserl, E. xii–xiii, xv–xx, xxii, xxiv, xxvi–xxvii, xxxi, xxxiii–xxxvi, xxxix, xlvi

idea 36, 90
idealism xiii, xliii, xlvi
   idealistic xiv, xix, xxiv, xliii, xlvi
ideational xliv–xlvi, 32, 37, 46–7, 79, 84
incoherent xxvii, xxx, 12, 15
indicative 2, 17, 64
individual xvi, xix, xxii, xxviii, xxx, xxxiii, xxxviii, xlii, xliv–xlv, xlvii–xlviii, li–lii, 17, 25, 36, 41–3, 49, 51, 55, 61, 66, 69–70, 85
individualization xlvii, 32–3, 35, 37, 51, 54, 56
   individualized xxviii, xxx, xxxv, xxxviii, xl–xli, 12, 14, 17, 36, 40, 43, 46, 49, 51, 53, 55–7

inductive xviii, 2, 17
inference xiii, 6–7, 94
infinite regress xxiv, 24, 28, 63, 72, 76
inherence xxv, xxvii, xxix, xl, 35, 37, 40, 44, 50
inorganic xiv, xl–xlii, 40
intentionality xv, xxii–xxxii, xxxiv, xl, lx, 8, 48
   intentionalized 35–6, 38, 41, 47, 51
introspection xvii–xviii, xx–xxi, li
   introspective xxvii–xviii, xx–xxi, xxvi, li, lv–lvi, 2, 12, 15, 54–5, 64, 75
intuition xix, xxvi
   intuited xviii, xix

James, W. xxxiii–xxxiv
Jaspers, K. xvi
judgment xxiii, 25–7, 41, 91

language xx, l, liv
law xxx, xli, 50, 63
   of depresentifcation 27, 45, 59, 76
   of temporality 44
   of temporalization 24–5, 27, 34
layer xxxii, xxxiv–xxxv, xxxvii–xxxviii, xl–xlii, xliv, l–li, lix, 54–5, 57–8, 61, 76, 78, 90–1

Maslow, A. H. 80
materialism 85
   material xxxiii, xlii, xliv–xlv, xlvii–xlviii, 9, 53, 86, 93
   materialistic 8, 13, 15, 85, 87, 90, 92, 94, 96
Mathews, F. xlviii
matter xiv, xxxix, xlii–xlv, 67
McDowell, J. xxvii
meditation xvii, li–lii, lx, 87

memorative xxxv, 26–8, 31, 45, 48, 54–5, 58–9, 61, 64–5, 68, 73–7, 90, 95–6
memory xxxiv, xxxvi–xxxvii, xlii, lv, 26, 28, 33, 44–6, 49–58, 61–2, 65, 69, 71–2, 75–6, 80, 84, 96
  layer xxxii, xxxiv–xxxv, xxxvii, xxxvii–xxxviii, l–li, 54–5, 58, 61
  representation l, 51–2, 72
  structure 46, 50–4, 56, 61, 76, 80
mental xxi–xxii, xxxv–xxxvii, xlii–xlv, xlvii–xlviii, liii, 64
  action liv–lv
  activity xix, xxiv, xxvi–xxvii, xxix–xxxii, xxxiv–xxxv, xxxix, xliv, li–lii, lv
Merleau-Ponty, M. xii, 64
metamorphosis xxv, xxvii, xxix, xl–xli, lix, lx, 2, 39–40, 43, 91
metaphysics xxxix, xlvi, xlviii
method xii–xv, xvii–xviii, xxi, xxiv–xxv, xlvi, li, 3, 17, 71
model 5, 79
movement 22–3, 25, 28, 67, 78, 95

Nagasawa, Y. xlvii–xlviii
naïve xxiv, xxix, xxxii, li, 18, 67, 76, 91, 96
  realism 18, 66, 72, 90, 94–5
natural attitude xviii, xxi–xxii, xxviii, xxxiv, xxxviii, l
non-conceptual xx, xxv–xxxiii, xxxv, xxxviii, xl, xlii–xliii, 11, 34, 37, 39, 46–7, 49
non-evidential xxv–xxx, 39, 45, 47, 48, 51, 59, 65, 67–9, 78, 85
  non-evident xxvi, 34–5, 39, 48
non-individualized 34, 36

object xii, xix–xxii, xxv–xxvi, xxviii–xxx, xxxii–xxxviii, xl–xliii, xlviii, lx, 5–7, 10, 13, 18–21, 23–8, 31, 37–8, 43–5, 55–7, 59, 65, 68–9, 71, 74–5, 78, 80, 95
objectification xlii, 26, 75
objectified xxviii, xxxii, 6–7, 33, 48, 60, 77–8, 90–1
objective xxx, xxxiv–xxxv, 6–8, 13, 15, 18, 20, 22–3, 25, 27, 35, 45, 54–5, 58–60, 63–8, 71–5, 78–80, 85, 91, 95
objectivity 11, 19, 21, 24, 26–9, 31, 45–5, 48, 53–4, 58, 64–5, 68, 72, 75, 77–8
objectness xxxiv, 23–6, 64
observation xvii, xviii–xxi, xxiii, xxv, xxix, xxxi–xxxii, xxxiv, xxxix–xlii, xlvi, xlviii, li–liv, lx, 2, 7, 12–13, 15, 17–21, 24–7, 29, 34–5, 39, 41, 45–6, 48–9, 52, 54–61, 64, 71–2, 74–6, 79, 84, 86, 94–6
ontology xii, xiv, xxxix, liv, 1
  ontic xxv, xxxiii, xl–xli, xlv, 48
  ontological xv, xvii, xxii, xxxix, xli–xlii, xlvii, xlix
organic xiv, xl–xlii, lx, 51
organization xvii, xxxv, xliii, xlv, 49, 53, 58, 62, 68, 94

panpsychism xlvi, xlviii
paradox of self-giving 14, 45, 72–3
paradoxical xix, xxvi, xxxiii, 64
participation xxxvii, xlv–xlvi, l, lix, 17, 23–4, 26, 32, 40–3, 50, 59, 63–6, 78, 84–5, 87–8, 95
parts xxxiii, xlvii, 10, 18, 20, 22, 55, 67–8
perception xxiii, xxx, xxxii, xxxvii–xxxviii, xl, lix, 13, 76, 80
  percept xxv, xxvii–xxviii, xl, lii, 5, 12, 14, 21–2, 42, 48, 64

perceptible xlii, 6, 12–14, 34–5, 38, 40, 46, 56–8, 60, 62, 64, 81
perceptual xvii, xxvii, xxxiv, xxxviii, xl–xlii, lv, 10–13, 20, 22, 36–7, 39, 42, 45, 47, 51, 53, 60, 78, 93, 95
physical xiv, xxx, xxxix, xlii, xliv, 79
physiological xxxv, xliii, 14–15, 53, 77
  theory 14, 20
Piaget, J. 13
Popper, K. R. xviii, 7
pre-given xxxiii–xxxiv, 8, 57–8, 76
pre-individualized 33, 35, 89
pre-reflective xix, xxxv, xlii
pre-universalized xxxvi
preconscious xix
predisposed xxxvii, 53, 57
presence xxxiv–xxxv, l, 24, 26–7, 58–61, 63–6, 68, 70–1, 74, 76–7, 90–1, 96
presentification 58–9
presupposition 5–7, 9, 13, 21, 28, 73, 79, 94
  presuppositionless 9, 15, 20
process xiii, xxiv–xxv, xxviii–xxx, xxxii, xxxiv–xxxvi, xxxviii, xli–xlii, xliv–xlv, lix, 2, 5–6, 11–12, 20–4, 26, 28–9, 35, 40, 44, 46, 49, 51–3, 55–7, 62, 65–6, 68–71, 73–9, 81, 88, 90–1, 94–5
  processual xix, xxvii, xxxiv–xxxv, xlvi, l–li, lv, 23, 65, 67
  processuality xxxiii, xxxviii, xliv, xlvii, 66–70
production xxx, 38, 46, 64, 66
  produce xxi, 9–10, 18, 78, 91
psychology xiii–xiv, xvi, xvii, xx–xxi, xxx, xxxvi, lii, lv–lvi, 2, 77

Quine, W. V. O. 1

Ramsey, F. P. 1
reality xix, xxix, xxxiii, xxxvii–xlvii, lix–lx, 5, 7–9, 12, 18, 23, 26, 38, 42–4, 49, 55, 58–9, 62, 64–7, 69, 72, 75, 77–80, 84–5, 87–8, 90–2, 93–6
rebound xxvii, xxxii, 48–9
reception xxx, liv, 88
  receive xiv, xvi, 10, 19, 32, 58, 60, 73, 77, 84, 86, 88
reciprocal l, 23, 52–3, 76–7
  determination xxvi–xxvii, 15, 32–3, 38–40, 47, 66, 78
recomposition xxviii, xxx, xxxv, xliii–xlvi, xlix, 67, 69
remembering 11, 27–8, 31, 33–4, 46, 49–54, 56–61, 63–4, 68, 71–7, 81, 89
  functional xxxvi, 71–2
  structural xxxvii, 28, 61, 71–2, 74, 96
representation xxiv, xxxii, xxxvii–xxxviii, xl, l, lix, 8, 11, 36, 51–2, 55–6, 58–9, 61–2, 66, 68–9, 72, 75–8, 96
Ribot, T. 50
Russell, B. xlvi, 14

Sartre, J. P. xii
Saussure, F. de 2
Schaffer, J. xlvii
science xii–xiv, xviii–xix, xxi, xlii, xlvi, liii, lix, lx, 1–3, 13, 18, 21, 29, 78–9, 85, 89–90, 92
self-apprehension 48, 55
self-consciousness xxx, 46
self-creating 62, 87
self-deception 61–2, 65–6, 72, 78, 90, 96
self-determination 23, 40, 46, 77, 87

self-explanatory xxviii, 14–15, 37, 44
self-formation 43, 77
self-giving xxviii, 18, 26–7, 45, 59–60, 63, 66, 72–4
self-realization 59, 62, 87, 91
selfish 58
Shani, I. xli, xlvii
Shapere, D. 8
Skinner, B. F. 5
sleep 58, 61–2
social xxvi, xvii, xxx, lvi, 70, 86, 92
spiritual xv, xlvi, 1, 43, 62, 66, 77, 79, 84–92, 94
Stegmüller, W. 2
Steiner, R. xv–xvi, xix, xxvi, xxxviii, xlii, xliv, xlvi, xlix–li, 1–2, 5, 9, 80, 85
stimulus xxvii, xxx–xxxi, xxxv, xxxviii, xl–xlii, xlv, 5–6, 60
stratification xv, xxxix, xli–xlii, 72, 77
structure of
　being 42–3
　consciousness xxvii, xxxvi
　reality 42–3
　remembering 50
　world (phenomena) 8, 43

Tarski, A. 14
temporal xliv, l, 32–4, 40, 44–6, 48, 59, 66, 68, 70, 75–6, 78–9
　extra-/non- xlviii, 32, 67–70
　sub- l, 44–6, 50, 52, 59–60, 76, 89–90
　super- xliv, xlvii, l, 32–4, 44–7, 50, 52, 59–60, 68, 70, 75–6, 78, 89–90

temporalization 18, 24–7, 33–4, 59–60, 68–71, 75, 78
thinking lvi, 14, 18, 31, 49, 61, 91, 94
　act xviii, xxvi–xxvii, xxxii, lii, 31–2, 46–7
　activity xxvii, 8, 32, 34, 46, 93
　thought content xviii, xxvi–xxvii, xxxii, lii, 15, 31–2, 42
totality xlvii, 32, 46
transition xxv–xxvi, xxix–xxxi, xxxv, xxxix–xl, 28–9, 36, 39–40, 42, 50, 70
truth xx, 1, 36, 44, 55, 58–61, 71–2, 96

unification 23, 46, 68, 84
　of percept and concept xxv, xxviii, xlii, xliv, 5, 10–11, 20–2, 42, 45, 48, 93
　of recollective dispositions 51, 65
　of thinking act and thought content xxxii, 42
universal xiii–xiv, xxvii–xxx, xxxiii–xxxv, xxxvii, xl, xlii–xliv, xlvi–xlviii, lx, 1, 10–12, 21, 32–4, 36, 39–40, 42–3, 46–8, 53–5, 56–8, 62, 66, 70, 79, 81, 85, 87, 90
universalization xxxiv, 46, 49–51, 53–7, 60, 64

wake lix, 45, 58, 61, 75, 91–2
Waldenfels, B. xxxi
Whitehead, A. N. 65
whole xli, xlvii–xlviii, 10, 24, 40, 55, 57, 67, 80–1, 88
Wittgenstein, L. xx

www.ingramcontent.com/pod-product-compliance
Lightning Source LLC
Chambersburg PA
CBHW061839300426
44115CB00013B/2444